ALIENATION AND FEMALE PSYCHE IN ANITA DESAI'S SELECTE NOVELS.

MRS. K. PREMAVATHI

To all my well-wishers

Contents

About The Author   *vii*

Acknowledgements   *ix*

1. Introduction   1

2. Cry, The Peacock   26

3. Bye- Bye, Blackbird   41

4. Where Shall We Go This Summer   51

5. Summing Up   64

Works Cited   87

About The Author

Premavathi Karuppanan is a Lecturer by profession. A naive writer tries to step in to the world of writing. She is also focussing on English Language Teaching. She is a soft skills trainer and serving the rural youth in terms id education. She is interested in public service and working with the an NGO called 'Aishwaryam Foundation'

Acknowledgements

Many writers are creators of their own piece of writing. But those creations will always have some backbones behind the work. I really feel thankful for all who have helped me to bring this book to publish. I would like thank Mrs. Anita Anbarasi, Dr. D. Vijayaraghavan and his students in specific.

CHAPTER ONE

INTRODUCTION

Even before Macaulay's famous recommendation for English education, and the British Government's subsequent decision on 7th march 1835 to implement English education in India, there was an eagerness to study English and use it in poetry and prose forms. The tensions created by the independence movement changed to a mood of relaxation when the object was achieved and politics ceased to be of primary interest. Gain of freedom and independence brought about the loss of certitude , aspiration and hope were replaced by merciless self-criticism, questioning and ironic assessment.

India is a vast country with different languages in different parts of the country. These regional languages differ from each other so much that it is not possible to communicate with people of other regions without a common language. Further, India is growing on all fronts whether it is social or economic angle. India is on the road to become a strong and prosperous nation in the world. India is trying to maintain a good foreign policy. For all this, there is need of a common language i.e., English. It is this language which is understood almost all over the region in addition to the national language Hindi. All schools and colleges teach English and mostly have it as the medium of instruction.

In today's world, we have to get knowledge of advanced technologies and all kinds of branches of Science. There is an urgent need of such a common language which can be understood by youth all over India and the language in which all data and information is available.

It is English only which can be rightly selected as the language to be studied by all of us from the very primary level. This language is a store house of social and political knowledge. Hence, study of English language is of great importance for a developing country like India. Without knowledge of this language, our technicians, mechanics and engineers cannot progress. In all international seminars or summits, all speeches or course material is in English. If India is to utilize these opportunities, and expand its universal view point, then English is the only language which should be learnt by all of us.

Though India is a one nation, it is a country with unity in diversity. We speak a dozens of different languages. For people belonging to different states, a common language is essential to communicate with each other and that is English. Further, a nation can remain intact only when its leaders can understand the people living in different regions and can communicate with them in effective and cordial manner. All leaders cannot understand more than three to five languages of various regions. However, they can easily understand the common language English. This language is important to inspire unity not only at the national level but also at the international level. To curb the separatist tendencies of our varied communities, we must continue to teach English. To survive in modern society, English knowledge is as essential as water.

Since the early 1600s, the English language has had a toehold on the Indian subcontinent, when the East India Company established settlements in Chennai, Kolkata, and Mumbai, formerly Madras, Calcutta, and Bombay respectively. The historical background of India is never far away from everyday usage of English. India has had a longer exposure to English than any other country which uses it as a second language, its distinctive words, idioms, grammar and rhetoric spreading gradually to affect all places, habits and culture.

In India, English serves two purposes. First, it provides a linguistic tool for the administrative cohesiveness of the country, causing people who speak different languages to become united. Secondly, it serves as a language of wider communication, including a large variety of different people covering a vast area. It overlaps with local languages in certain spheres of influence and in public domains.

Generally, English is used among Indians as a 'link' language and it is the first language for many well-educated Indians. It is also the second language for many who speak more than one language in India.

A positive attitude to the study of English is essential to the integration of people into Indian society. There would appear to be virtually no disagreement in the community about the importance of English language skills. Using English one will become a citizen of the world almost naturally. English plays a dominant role in the media. It has been used as a medium for inter-state communication and broadcasting both before and since India's independence. India is, without doubt, committed to English as a national language. The impact of English is not only continuing but increasing.

After Independence, India became a nation state, and it was intended that English would gradually be phased out as the language of administration. But there was no simple solution as to which language should replace it. At first Hindi, the most widely spoken language, seemed the obvious choice, but following violent protests in 1963 in the state of Tamil Nadu against the imposition of Hindi as a national language, opinion has remained divided. In a country with over 900 million people and more than a thousand languages, it is difficult to choose a single national language, as mother tongue speakers of that language would automatically enjoy greater social status and have easier access to positions of power and influence.

Even Gandhi accepted that his message was most widely understood if expressed in English. So, although English is not an indigenous language, it remains as an 'Associate Language' in India, alongside Hindi, the 'Official Language of the Union of India' and eighteen 'National Languages', such as Bengali, Gujarati and Urdu, that have a special status in certain individual states.

Indian English is a distinct variety of the English language. Many Indians claim that it is very similar to British English, but this opinion is based on a surface level examination of lexical similarities. Of course, one must keep in mind that not every linguistic item is used by every Indian English speaker and that a great deal of regional and educational differentiation exists. Even so, items can be identified which are indicative of Indian English speech and which are widely used. These operate on various phonological, morphological, lexical, and syntactic levels, resulting in the formation of a new level of English language in India.

U.N. has recognized five languages as its official languages and of them English takes the first position because of its background, international acclaim of easy access to the people. If we go back to historical facts, we see that half of the globe was under the British imperialism. Those countries coming directly under British rule had by necessity or under compulsion to learn English and the rest either being influenced by the English culture or to keep pace with modern trend had but to opt for learning it.

Indian writing in English has a relatively short but highly charged history .It started with the advent of East India Company in India. It all started in the summer of 1608 when Emperor Jahangir, in the courts of Mughals, welcomed Captain William Hawkins, Commander of British Naval Expedition ,Hector. It was India's first tryst with an Englishman and English. Jahangir later allowed Britain to open a permanent port and factory on the special request of King James IV that was conveyed by his ambassador Sir Thomas Roe. English were here to stay.

The East India Company spread its wings in southern peninsula and English language started to get newer pockets of influence. But it was still time for the first English book to capitalize. Late 17th century saw the coming of printing press in India but the publications were largely confined to either printing Bible or government decrees. Then came newspapers. It was in 1779 that the first English Newspaper named Hickey's Bengal Gazette was published in India. The breakthrough in Indian English literature came in 1793 A.D. when a person by the name of Sake Dean Mahomet published a book in London titled *Travels of Dean Mahomet*. This was essentially Mahomet's travel narrative that can be put somewhere between a Non-Fiction and a Travelogue.

Indian English writers were a group of English educated Indians who wrote in English and whose native or co-native language could be one of the numerous languages of India. It is also associated with the works of the members of the Indian Diaspora. It is frequently referred to as Indo-Anglian literature. As a category, this production comes under the broader realm of postcolonial literature- the production from previously colonized countries such as India.

This researcher would like to focus on the root and brief literary history of Indian writing in English and the genre – novel in Indo-Anglian literature up to the time of Anita Desai for better understanding of her novels. Here, it is essential to mention the brief history of Indian writing in English and the contributors of it. Along with the list of the contributors in Indian writing in English, the rise of the new form of literature- novel in India is also necessary to focus.

For that researcher would like to divide the history of Indian writing in English into three parts, first to understand the beginning and exploration of Indian writing in English by major contributors, second for the rise and development of new literary genre (novel) in Indo-Anglian literature and third to understand Anita Desai as a novelist. These three parts are foundation of this research work. On the basis of the understanding of the Indo-Anglian literature and the rise and development of novel in Indo-Anglian literature, and the rising feministic consciousness in *Cry, the Peacock* and *Where Shall We Go This Summer*, Anita Desai's novels can be judged properly.

In its early stages, the Indian writings in English were heavily influenced by the Western art form of the novel. It was typical for the early Indian English language writers to use English unadulterated by Indian words to convey experiences that were primarily Indian. The core reason behind this step was the fact that most of the readers were either British or British educated Indians. In the coming century, the writings were largely confined to writing history chronicles and government gazettes.

In the early 20th century, when the British conquest of India was achieved, a new breed of writers started to emerge on the block. These writers were essentially British who were born or brought up or both in India. Their writing consisted of Indian themes and sentiments but the way of storytelling was primarily western.. This group consisted likes of Rudyard Kipling, Jim Corbett and George Orwell among others. Books such as *Kim, The JungleBook, 1984, Animal Farm* and *The man-eaters of Kumaon* etc were liked and read all over the English-speaking world. In fact, some of the writings of that era are still considered to be the masterpieces of English Literature. In those periods, natives were represented by the likes of Rabindra Nath Tagore and Sarojini Naidu. In fact, *Geetanjali* helped Tagore win Nobel Prize for Literature in the year 1913

In 1793, Sake Dean Mahomed wrote perhaps the first book by an Indian in English, called *The Travels of Dean Mahomed*. However, most early Indian writing in English was non-fictional work, such as biographies and political essays. Recognition of the country as one in the world community increased Indian writers' self confidence, and they assumed the role of critics both of past and present instead of merely voicing his times, as the previous writers had done. This began to change in the late 1800s, when famous Indian authors who wrote mostly in their mother tongue, began to try their hand at writing in English. In the early 1900s, Rabindranath Tagore began translating his works from Bengali to English.

Ever since the publication of Bankim Chandra Chaterjee's novel *Rajmohan's Wife* in1864, the Indian novel in English has grown by leaps and bounds in respect of bulk, variety and maturity. After the World War I, the Indian English novel became determinedly more realistic and less idealized.

Soon after, a new generation of Indian authors, who wrote almost exclusively in English, hit the bookshelves, beginning in 1935 with R.K. Narayan's *Swami and Friends* and Mulk Raj Anand's *Untouchable*. Raja Rao's *Kanthapura* followed in 1938.they were known as 'The Big Three'. They shaped the destiny of Indian English fiction. What made Narayan's, Anand's and Rao's writing different from the Indian authors before them was that their stories were about the contemporary man on the street. There was also an Indianness to their work, in terms of the words they used and their style of writing. This resonated with the new, but growing ranks of Indians reading English literature. Their works were the forerunners to the magnificent diversity of Indian writing in English that we see today.

Indian English literature is the outcome of the cross fertilization of two fruitful cultures-Indian and English. It is literature created by Indians both before and after independence. All Indian writers who wrote in English since the days of Raja Ram Mohan Roy down to our own time belong to Indian English literature. It spontaneously and powerfully expresses varying shades of emotions, thoughts and feelings typical to the genius and character of India

Anand, R.K. Narayan and Raja Rao, distinguished not only for their own work but as the inaugurators of the form itself since it was they who defined the area in which the Indian novel in English was to operate, drew the first models of its characters and themes and elaborated its particular logic. "Each used its own version of English freed from the foggy taste of Britain". (Walsh, 62)

The majority of Mulk Raj Anand's (1905 - 2004) novels brings to the limelight the inequalities of society and trials and tribulations of the less fortunate, *Untouchable(1935)*, *Coolie(1936)*, *The Village(1939)*, and *The Private Life of an Indian Prince(1953)* address the evils existing in the society in the Marxist terms. His novels also give a graphic description of the daily existence of his characters, their tale of woe, sweat and misery. *Untouchable (1935)* targets the evil of casteism and brings to the surface the issue of segregation of people on the basis of their profession.

In *Coolie (1936),* he presents a poverty-stricken protagonist. Munoo, who portrays the hollowness of the society and the curse faced by the proletariat. He was instrumental in bringing about an awareness of the inequality that existed in India. He also advocated solutions for the issues. He is one of the first Indian writers in English to have gained international readership with his first novel *Untouchable* published in 1935. His other notable works include *The Village, Coolie,* and *The Private Life of an IndianPrince.*

Though historically Indian English fiction owes its origin to Bankim Chandra Chatterjee's *Rajmohan's Wife* (1864), its foundation was laid by Mulk Raj Anand when he published his *Untouchable* in 1935. R.K. Narayan and Raja Rao joined him in giving, as it were, 'a local habitation and a name' to Indian English fiction in nineteen thirties.

Anand's *Untouchable* and *Coolie,* Narayan's *Swami and Friends* and *The Bachelor of Arts,* Raja Rao's *Kanthapura* mark the beginning of IndianEnglish fiction. And these three novelists continued to write till the end of the twentieth century. Anand was always for highlighting indigenous culture, art and Anand's important novels include *Untouchable* (1935), *Coolie* (1936), *Two Leaves and a Bud* (1937), *The Village* (1939), *Across the Blackwaters* (1941), *The Big Heart* (1945), *Seven Summers* (1951), *The Private Life of an Indian Prince* (1953), *Gauri* (1960), *Morning Face* (1968), *Confessions of a Lover* (1976), *The Bubble* (1984), *Little Plays of Mahatma Gandhi* (1991) and *Nine Moods of Bharata: Novel of a Pilgrimage* (1998).

Social realism is the major concern in his works. He has brought innovations in fiction by making an untouchable the hero or anti-hero of his first novel, *Untouchable*. Anand takes characters from contemporary life who have been deprived of their rights by the oppressors. His Marxist leanings are unmistakable. A person who lived more than twenty years abroad during his youth, unlike the contemporary diasporic writers was never in search of 'home'. 'Home' was uppermost in his mind and deeply engraved in his heart. Hence, he never lost touch with Indian reality and social conditions. Of Anand's fiction, Anna Rutherford writes: "Anand's characters invariably fall into three classes: the victims who are usually the protagonists; the oppressors, those who oppose change and progress, and the goodmen." (R.K.Rarayan's Novels: A mix of Myth and Reality, P 145)

His other notable works include *"The Village"*, *"Coolie"*, and *"The Private Life of an Indian Prince"*. Mulk Raj is one author whose every book is highly recommended. He is one of the first Indian writers in English to have gained international readership with his first novel "Untouchable" published in 1935. His other notable works include *"The Village"*, *"Coolie"*, and *"The Private Life of an Indian Prince.*

Raja Rao was a respected and honoured Indian writer of English novels and short stories. His works have always been deeply rooted in Hinduism, mirrored all through by the man himself. Raja Rao's semi - autobiographical novel, *'The Serpent and the Rope'* (1960), is a story of the seeking of spiritual consciousness in Europe and India. The novel had established Raja Rao as one of the finest Indian stylists.

Raja Rao was born on November 8, 1908 in Hassan, in the state of Mysore (presently Karnataka) in South India, into a well-known Brahmin (Hoysala Karnataka) household. He was the eldest of nine siblings, amongst his two brothers and seven sisters. Raja Rao's mother tongue was Kannada. Raja Rao's father served as a teacher of Kannada in Nizam's College, in what was the then Hyderabad State. The death of his mother, when the Indian English Litterateur was barely four, left an eternal impression upon Raja Rao. The non-existence of a mother and what it is like to live like an orphan have made new themes in his work.

Raja Rao had his education in Muslim institutions, the Madarsa-e- Aliya in Hyderabad and the Aligarh Muslim University. His interest in French had developed during his learning years and he began to learn French at the Aligarh University itself. After passing out matriculation in 1927, Raja Rao went back to Hyderabad and studied for his degree at Nizam's College. After graduating from Madras University, having obtained major degrees in English and History, he won the Asiatic Scholarship of the Government of Hyderabad in 1929. The scholarship was meant for students who would leave the country to study abroad. His initial stories were published in French and English. During the period of 1931-1932, the writer donated four articles written in Kannada for Jaya Karnataka, a powerful journal.

Rao's second novel, _The Serpent and the Rope_ (1960), considered his masterpiece, is a philosophical and somewhat abstract account of a young intellectual Brahman and his wife seeking spiritual truth in India, France, and England; it plays on the dialogue between Orient and Occident. His other novels are the allegorical *The Cat and Shakespeare: A Tale of India* (1965); *Comrade Kirillov* (1976), an examination of communism; and *The Chessmaster and His Moves* (1988), which is peopled by characters from various cultures seeking their identities. Rao's short stories were collected in *The Cow of the Barricades and Other Stories* (1947) and *The Policeman and the Rose* (1978). He also wrote *The Great Indian Way: A Life of Mahatma Gandhi* (1998).

Raja Rao's best-known novels include his first, "Kanthapura," published in England in 1938 and in the United States by New Directions in 1963. Narrated in the voice of an elderly woman, the novel explores the turbulence in a South Indian village caused by the arrival of a Gandhi-like figure who preaches nonviolent resistance to British rule. Written when Raja Rao was just 21 and published only years later, *Kanthapura* reveals his characteristic style - lyrical, fluid, and colloquial - already firmly in place.

R.K. Narayan incontrovertibly is one of the most famous writers in India, perhaps the most well known and commented upon Indian English writer. His chronicling of the life at the "back of beyond" township of Malgudi has been recognized as a unique attempt to create the outer framework of a regional novel which essentially captures the spirit of humanity in general and India in particular. He told stories of simple folks trying to live their simple lives in a changing world. He is a traditional teller of tales, a creator of realist fiction which is often gentle, humorous and warm rather than hard hitting or profound. Life for R.K. Narayan is the greatest teacher. Most of his characters are in quest of inner peace and freedom from the collective.

R.K.Narayan is a penetrating analyst of human passions and human motives, which makes him a great critic of human conduct. He presents both the good and the evil and never takes sides. He holds a mirror to nature, and like a mirror shows nature truthfully without any distortion. Despite this, he does take the pain to communicate that bad or evil actions lead to similar consequences and good actions yield good results. There is no doubt that R.K.Narayan's vision is essentially moral, for the problems he sets himself to resolve in his novels are largely ethical. Besides, it usually revolves around Hindu traditionalism in Narayan's works, and involves a confrontation when that traditionalism is defied by the characters that entertain a more modern and more guilelessly individualistic values.

R.K.Narayan's main characters resist the traditional, religious and familial duties and then inadvertently drift towards their destined doom because in Narayan's system the aberration or disorder caused by the non-adherence of norms definitely leads to adverse outcomes. However, as stated R.K.Narayan's moral vision is not consciously or explicitly cultivated in his writing. They are incidentally and inherently part of his art of storytelling and of the cultural environment, which is the background for all his stories. Thus, Narayan's message in his writings has to be garnered by the readers themselves according to their own respective intuitions.

R.K.Narayan's knowledge of Indian classical literature, philosophy, religion, morals and ethics pervades his writing, but as said already he does not burden unnecessarily, his readers with discourses on his viewpoint and vision.. So behind the narrative mask of his novels, R.K. Narayan attempts to portray a vision of life, a life of opposing dualities, of appearance and reality, beliefs and betrayals. According to S. C. Sharma and Birendra Kumar, "Narayan uses myth as a technique to illustrate his moral vision of life. More interestingly, he always comes upon an ancient myth which enables him to express his view of the world and vision of life" (P 145). For instance, "Raju, in re-enacting the penances of the sages of yore, is trying to bring rain to end the drought. This is reminiscent of the story of the sage-king Bhagirath who conducted severe penance to bring down the goddess Ganga, a story found in both the Ramayana and Matsyapurana" (Sen 24).

The setting for most of Narayan's stories is the fictional town of Malgudi, first introduced in *Swami and Friends*. His narratives highlight social context and provide a feel for his characters through everyday life. He has been compared to William Faulkner, who also created a fictional town that stood for reality, brought out the humour and energy of ordinary life, and displayed compassionate humanism in his writing. Narayan's short story writing style has been compared to that of Guy de Maupassant, as they both have an ability to compress the narrative without losing out on elements of the story. Narayan's major work include *Swami and Friends* (1935, *The Bachelor of Arts* (1937) ,*The Dark Room* (1938), *The English Teacher* (1945),*Mr. Sampath* (1948),*The Financial Expert* (1952),*Waiting for the Mahatma* (1955),*The Guide* (1958).

Narayan won numerous awards during the course of his literary career. His first major award was in 1958, the Sahitya Akademi Award for *The Guide*. When the book was made into a film, he received the Filmfare Award for the best story. In 1964, he received the Padma Bhushan during the Republic Day honours. In 1980, he was awarded the AC Benson Medal by the (British) Royal Society of Literature, of which he was an honorary member. In 1982 he was elected an honorary member of the American Academy of Arts and Letters. He was nominated for the Nobel Prize in Literature multiple times, but never won the honour.

Recognition also came in the form of honorary doctorates by the University of Leeds (1967), the University of Mysore (1976) and Delhi University (1973). Towards the end of his career, Narayan was nominated to the upper house of the Indian Parliament for a six-year term starting in 1989, for his contributions to Indian literature. A year before his death, in 2001, he was awarded India's second-highest civilian honour, the Padma Vibhushan.

Khushwant Singh, perhaps India's best known journalist was born in 1915 in Hadali, in Punjab. He was educated at Government College, Lahore and at King's College and the Inner Temple in London. He began his career as a journalist with the All India Radio in 1951.

Khushwant Singh was an illustrious storywriter, historian, political writer, essayist, biographer, translator, novelist and journalist. Since independence he has been the country's most well- known English writer. In Indian literary history Khushwant Singh's name is bound to evolve as one of the finest historians and novelists, a forthright political commentator, and an outstanding observer and social critic. He is attributed with freethinking. He brought history to our doorsteps and quite ideally therefore India describes him as "The Capital's best known living monument". Apart from his literary works, his roles as a lawyer, diplomat, critic, journalist, novelist, humorist, naturalist and politician made Khushwant Singh a man larger than life.

His journalistic career started with his stint in *Yojana* as an editor. However, major breakthrough in his journalistic career came in 1969 when he was offered editorship of *The Illustrated Weekly of India. The Weekly* brought him name, fame and money. The 'Editor's Page' came to be a widely read column.. In 1975, he received Padma Bhushan in recognition of his contribution to Journalism and Literature.

In his political writings, the subjects he touches upon range from communalism and elections to political ideology and political system. In fact, he writes prolifically on elections, administration, communalism, secularism, prohibition, emergency, human rights, democracy, nationalism, international relations, Pakistan, political ideology and political system. He is a votary of democracy as an instrument of people's empowerment, particularly that of the socially and politically marginalized. However, Khushwant Singh's was the lone voice in support of emergency as he thought it to be the only way out for imposing disciplined work culture directed at family planning and slum clearance. His remarks become most poignant in the aftermath of 1984 anti Sikhs riots. Khushwant Singh has had a very successful career as a writer. Among the works he has published are a classic two-volume *History of the Sikhs*, several novels (the best-known of which are *Train toPakistan* and *The Company of Women*), and a number of translated works and non-fiction books on

Delhi, nature and current affairs.

> *"The radical feminists allege that marriage is at the very*
> *Root of woman's subjection to the man because through*
> *It man controls both her reproduction and her person."*

(*Faces of feminism*, P 230)

Feminism is a collection of movements and ideologies aimed at defining, establishing and defending equal political, economic and social rights for women. French Philosopher Charles Fourier is credited with having originated the word in 1837. It is a global and revolutionary ideology as well as a socio-cultural movement that aims at the freedom of woman from male domination in the patriarchal society. It highlights various hidden and oppressive aspects of man – woman relationship. It has a profound impact on the debate concerning the relation between genders, culture and creativity and knocks down the claims of certain cultures, which believe that woman can only produce children and not art.

The rise of Feminism as a movement on the continent began with the crucial question that portrayal of women by male artists must be deficient for; even the most imaginative of male writers is by no means equipped to give an authentic rendering of the female sensibility. Of late there has been a tendency among the women Indian novelists writing in English to share this view. There has emerged a group of women novelists who try to give their own side of the story from their own point of view.

Women have always been the subject of literary work but literature has mostly been created by men. A genuine question that arises is how much men know about feminine psyche. And even if they know much or little how far is it true? Psychologists too believe that the male carries some rudiments of the female. Medical science informs us that there is no gender difference in the beginning. It is only later that they assume gender characteristics. But more important are the psychic characteristics. Women writers of all ages have a natural preference for writing about women characters. Such preference may be a limitation to their creativity, as the case of Jane Austen who excels in her two inches of ivory.

Traditionally Indian women have been treated as marginalized lot. They were represented as spineless, wooden creature, subjected to male domination. The laws of Manu dictated the position of women in the family and society. Women were never allowed to be independent and had to spend life under the authority of a man. The sublimation and suppression of natural desires and aspirations creates a deep struggle in women. The position of women has always been reflected in the novels written by Indian women writers in English. They capture the intricacies of the problems of women caught between the two worlds of tradition and modernity. Mostly, they deal with women's suffering and the pathetic plight of women under male domination.

The first category of feminist writers consists of writers like Jane Austen, Bronte Sisters and others. The second category includes writers like Emily Dickinson, Virginia Woolf, Sylvia Plath and many others. The first category of writers have struggled to be simply acknowledged by the intelligentia while the second group has revolted against the male oriented society and sought to establish an isolated world away from the males. The third group has maintained a balance between the above two extremes by being both feminine and feminist at the same time. This group of writers have also less talked about the social or political freedom and never visualized a world existing without men. Kamala Das is a part of this third category.

The emergence of women novelists in Indian English literature took place as early as the last quarter of the nineteenth century. But, it was only after independence, that they could make solid contribution to Indian English fiction. The post-Independence period, has brought to the forefront a number of noted women novelists who have enriched Indian English fiction by a creative release of feminine sensibility. The woman has been the focus of many literary works in this period. Writers like Kamala Markandaya, Nayantara Sahgal, Ruth Prawer Jhabvala, Anita Desai and Shashi Deshpande have achieved recognision of recent times.

Problems of women which were till now in the periphery have now shifted to the centre. Through the eyes of these women writers, we get a glimpse of a different world till now not represented in literature. Women, who were till then treated as second class citizens were assigned their due place in these novels. The potential of human achievement can be realized though their writings. Without assessing the work done by these writers, no critic can gather the implication of Indian English fiction. These novels present a picture of the impact of education on women, her new status in the society and her assertion of individuality. The works of Indian women novelists like Anita Desai and Shashi Deshpande can be compared with those of the Canadian novelists like Margaret Atwood,

Margaret Lawrence and Aritha Van Herk. All these writes write of life as seen by women and life as affecting women.

One of the reasons that women have, in such large number, taken up their pen is because it has allowed them to create their own world. It has allowed them to set the conditions of existence free from the direct interference of men. Similarly many women have taken to reading women's writing because from which they can explore a wide range of experience of the world from which they can identify with a range of characters and a variety of existences. That is why women's writing has occupied such a significant and central place in women's lives.

Once the silent spectator, puppet in the hands of man, the theme of major part of literature, the centre of attraction and importance 'the woman' took the new instrument, the unfamiliar weapon, 'the pen' into her hands and started wielding it slowly, steadily and successfully ever since. Thanks to the feminist movement which extended its strong, firm helping hand for 'the Women' to wriggle herself free from the quicksand of 'male domination'. Some of the eminent women writers in this category include Kamala Markandaya, Shashi Deshpande, Anita Desai, Arundhati Roy. They have risen to celebrity and won global recognition in literature. The fictional world of Kamala Markandaya is thematically wide as her concern is social, economic, cultural and sometimes historical rural life, poverty, hunger, fear ,despair and deaths are her recurrent themes. Her themes and concerns are typical in *Nectar in a Sieve*. In this her concern is hunger and inner corruption that is anticipated through hunger. She presents a realistic picture of the impact of industrialization on rural India.

Kamala Markandaya effectively presents, the predicament of women in her novels. Her Rukmani, no doubt is a triumph of the spirit of tradition. She is the arche type, the ideal idolized and adored woman of Indian tradition. Rural life is like nectar in a sieve. *The Nowhere Man and Nectar in a sieve* form two of the major works of Markandaya.

Shashi Deshpande is another prominent writer belonging to this era. Her novels present a social world of many complex relationships. In her novels many men and women living together, journeying across life in their different roles. She represents modern Indian women's search for definitions about the self and society, and the relationships that are central to women. *A matter of Time* (1996) her masterpiece novel clearly shows her eagerness to concentrate on larger issues pertaining to human life.

Her first full length novel, *Roots and Shadows* deals with the protagonist Indu's painful self-analysis. Her important novels include *The Dark Holds No Terrors (1980), Roots and Shadows and That Long Silence.*

Arundhati Roy emerged on the international fictional scene by her first novel, *The God of Small Things(1997)*, a Booker prize winner book in October, 1997. The novel can undoubtedly be called the book of the decade. The Booker citation describes the novel as one written with extraordinary linguistic inventiveness. *The God of Small Things* is the truthful portrayal of the plight of women in society and their strenuous struggle to be recognized as a human being in the male dominated conservative world. Every inch of life of an Indian woman is filled with multifaceted struggles. Life, for a deserted woman Ammu in Ahrudhati Roy's *The God of Small Things* offers no choice except endless suffering.

My novels are no reflection of Indian society, politics, or character. They are part of my private effort to seize upon the raw material of life-its shapelessness, its meaninglessness.

(Anita Desai. The Book I Enjoyed Most P 24)

Anita Desai like Joyce and Woolf is widely recognized as the pioneer of psychological novel in modern Indian English literature. She penetrates psychologically deep into the inner working of women and externalizes their passive reaction. In his respect she approximates to Dostoevsky, Proust, Virginia Woolf, James Joyce and Henry James.

Born in Mussoorie on the 24th june 1937 of mixed parentage a Bengali father and a German mother, she was to be benefited by the diverse influences which led to the fermentation of her poetic imagination. At a tender age of seven, she began to write prose, and published some small pieces in children's magazine. She had her education-first at Queen Mary's school, and then at Miranda House, Delhi University, where she took her Bachelor's degree in English literature in 1957.

Anita Desai has several books to her credit which include *Cry, the Peacock* (1963), *Voices in the City* (1965), *Bye-Bye Blackbird* (1971), *Where shall we go this summer?* (1975), *Fire on the Mountain* (1977), (for which she won Royal Society of Literature's of Letters Award, *The Village by the Sea* (1982) *In Custody* (1984), (which was short listed for the 1984 Booker Prize). *Baumgartner's Bombay* (1988) and her latest novel *Journey To Ithaca*. Desai's short stories have been collected under the title *Games of Twilight* (1978). Besides these novels, her review articles and interviews are considered to be the epitomes of fictional interest and flavour.

Desai's characters are intense, self absorbed, even morbidly so, possessed by a conscience that never allows them peace of mind, constantly analyzing, probing and questioning, merciless in its passion for introspection.

Cry, the peacock is the story of an Indian woman Maya who undergoes considerable traumatic experiences obsessed by forebodings and mental tension. In this novel Anita explores the turbulent emotional world of the neurotic protagonist Maya, who is constantly haunted by a presentiment of her husband's death on account of her belief in astrological prediction. She desperately looks for someone to ward off the shadow of imminent death but none realizes her exuberance of sentiment, emotion and tension.

The novel begins with Maya's reaction to the death of her pet dog and husband's total indifference to her. Anita projects the psychic mind of an Indian woman in the tone of Maya. Maya absorbs herself in her inner world of tragic vision.

In the Second novel *Voices in the City,* Anita Desai psychoanalyses the inner mind of three characters Nirod Ray and his sisters Monisha and Amla. These characters feel utterly frustrated like Maya of the novel *Cry thePeacock.* They profess a mysterious longing to return home in Kalipong and enjoy the solitude and serenity of jungles but they are forced to live in Calcutta which is a city of despair and death for them. Since we are concerned in this paper with the psychological exploitation of women's mind we turn our attention to the character of Maya, Sita, Sarah of *Cry The Peacock, Where ShallWe Go This Summer,* and *Bye-Bye, Blackbird* respectively.

In *Where Shall We Go This Summer,* Anita follows the track of Bronte sisters, who chose to study the heart and mind of women's point of view. Their novels provide glimpses into the tortured souls of their heroines. In like manner Anita too portrays the tragic intensity of her women characters with a feminist perspective. The novel *Where Shall We Go This Summer* depicts the tragic life of Sita who leads a life of isolation and loneliness in her husband's house. Her unmitigated suffering drives her to a state of madness and desperation.

The next novel *Fire on the Mountain* explores the inner emotional world of Nanda Kaul and Raka. Anita Desai draws a picture of the tragedy of Nanda leading a segregated life like a recluse in a lonely hill hut. In *The Clear Light of Day*, Vimla's attitude is more or less similar to that of Nanda in the sense that she too prefers to lead a solitary life in a decaying house.

In Anita Desai's *Bye- Bye,Black Bird* the western figure Sarah marries an Indian working in London. Sarah living on two different planes playing two roles, struggles for an indentity leaving her in a state of loneliness. Cultural alienation place a vital role in this novel.

Alienation is one of the greatest problems confronting the modern Man. It is the same portrayed by Anita Desai in a very systematic way through the character of Hugo Baumgartner, which makes a significant landmark in her career. It is a novel which unfolds against the backdrop of the Second World War. It is a complete departure from her earlier novels. Our present study is to analyse the alienation and psychological aspects of women characters in Anita Desai's three prominent novels. The novel *Cry, the Peacock* has been selected for study and is discussed in chapter 2, the third chapter deals with Desai's novel *Bye-Bye, Blackbird*, and the third chapter is on *Where Shall We Go this Summer*.

Anita Desai has added a new dimension to Indo-Anglian fiction by concentrating on the exploration of the troubled psyche of her characters, especially, the women in particular. The women writers in Indo-Anglian fiction have shown greater understanding and strength to dig deep into the psyche of the Indian characters. She has depicted through her characters, feminine personality and feminine psyche better than other Indo-Anglian novelists.

CHAPTER TWO

CRY, THE PEACOCK

Cry, the Peacock is the story of an Indian woman Maya who undergoes considerable traumatic experiences obsessed by forebodings and mental tension. In this novel Anita Desai explores the turbulent emotional world of the neurotic Protagonist Maya, who is constantly haunted by a presentiment of her husband's death on account of her belief in astrological prediction. She desperately looks for someone to ward off the shadow off the imminent death but none realizes her emotional state of sentiment, emotion and tension. Even her husband Gautama, an insensible and unsentimental youth, hardly shares in her psychological suffering. On the contrary, he treats her as a spoilt child.

Cry, the Peacock brings with Maya's reaction to the death of her Pet dog and husband's total indifference to her. Desai projects the psychic mind of an Indian woman in the tone of Maya. She Says, "He was not on my side at all, But across a river, across a mountain, and would always remain so" (*Cry, the Peacock*, 131). Maya absorbs herself in her inner world of tragic vision. The husband-wife alienation caused by the temperamental incompatibility between the two, an important existentialist theme – forms the very core of the novel.

With the rising popularity of the science of psychology in the twentieth century, fiction writers in the West began to depict the inner psyche of the characters in their novels. The popularity of this genre of novel began to attract the attention of the Indian English prose fiction writers. With the publication of Anita Desai's first novel, *Cry, the Peacock*, in 1963, the stream-of- consciousness novel came into its own in India. However, one cannot ignore the fact that novelists prior to Desai had depicted the interior landscapes of the minds of their characters in their novels but in bits and pieces and not as the main theme of their novels. Seeing the success of Desai, many other Indian novelists followed her footsteps and brought out excellent novels of this genre. Nevertheless, Desai was the harbinger of the stream-of- consciousness novel in India, the one who caused its 'dawn' here.

Gautama is pragmatic, unromantic, unsentimental and believes in 'detachment' on every account. Maya on the other hand, is a highly sensitive creature gifted with poetic imagination and a neurotic sensibility. The death of Toto which upsets. Maya is nothing to Gautama. This is suggestive of the lack of any possible emotional communication between them. Communication gap between husband and wife is felt throughout the novel. Maya and Gautama disagree with each other even over trifles. Although their marriage has been a complete failure, they continue to be together, leading a mechanical life. Maya herself reflects upon her marriage which has become a misalliance.

> "*It was discouraging to reflect as how much in our marriage was based upon a nobility forced upon us from outside, and, therefore, neither, true nor*

> *lasting, it was broken repeatedly, and repeatedly the*
> *pieces were picked up and put together again.*
> *(Cry, the Peacock P 45)* "

Unable to establish a rapport with her husband and to find a meaning in her 'arid existence', Maya remains throughout an utterly lonely-creature in this helpless and indifferent world. Maya suffers from father fixations. She marries Gautama who is much older and a friend of her father, and for her he serves perhaps, as a father –surrogate. Her neurosis is the result of her love-wish which she transfers from her father to her husband and which remains unfulfilled. Her neurosis is further heightened by her awareness of her horoscope and the macabre prediction of the albino astrologer, which leads to her killing Gautama and her committing suicide. In spite of her neurosis, Maya commands sympathy of the readers because she reminds one of Henrik Ibsen's Nora of *A Doll's House*: "Our Homes' been nothing but a laypen I've been your doll-wife here, just I was papa's doll-child" (*A Doll's House*, vol. 1-110)

In this novel Desai has dealt with a sterile woman, the pampered child, and is brought up in an atmosphere of luxury. She lives, to use her own words, like "a toy prince in a toy world". Her Pet dog Toto's death, who resembles as a child to Maya, makes her neurosis worse, but Gautama a practical man takes this event easy and makes arrangement for its burial, consoles Maya in his own way and says that he would bring another dog for her.

This novel shows the real cause of disrupter in marriage of Maya and Gautama. The novel is about Maya's cry for love and relationship in her loveless wedding with Gautama. The peacock's cry is symbolic of Maya's cry for love and understanding. The marital discord results from the temperamental disparity between Gautama and Maya. Even Maya's childlessness exaggerates her agony of loneliness which she feels in spite of being married. She becomes highly sensitive as a result of it. Maya wants to enjoy life to the utmost.

She enjoys beautiful sights and sounds. She is an epicurean to the core. In contrast, she is married to Gautama, a friend of her father very senior to her age and a prosperous middle aged lawyer. He is a kindly, cultured, rational, practical and busy with his own affair of business. He looks upon her love for good things as nothing more than sentimentalism and once makes a disparaging remark about her that she has a mind of third rate poetess.

Maya longs for companionship which to her despair she never finds in her marriage. The novel echoes in the cry of Maya the desire of a married woman to be loved with passion which few tend to get. "Because when you are away from me, I want you. Because I insist on being with you and being allowed to touch you and know you. You can't bear it, can you? No, you are afraid, you might perish" (p.113). On another occasion, in spite of her seductive postures, Gautama remains rigid and cold; Maya herself describes her predicament in these words: "I turned upon my side, close to him, conscious of the swell of my hip that rose under the white sheet which fell in sculptured folds about my rounded forms" (pp.41-42). Thus she doesn't remain emotionally but physically dissatisfied too.

In Anita Desai's novel, there is a shift from the collective to the personal, from the communal to the individual. Unlike Jhabvala's novels where the social dimension is more important than the characters, and Markandaya's novels where the stress is on the economic and social background, Desai's novels highlight individual characters:

their inner worlds and sensibilities. Her first two novels. *Cry, thePeacock* and *Voices in the City* are said to have ushered in the psychological novel in Indian English fiction.

We get scores of such examples throughout the novel, where Gautama neglects emotional yearnings of Maya. Though they live together, Gautama knows very little about her. In order to console her, he offers a cup of tea without realizing Maya's shattered state of mind. This mechanical gesture only makes her to brood over Gautama's insensitivity:

> *"Showing how little he knew of my misery, or how to comfort me. But then, he knew that concerned me. Giving me an opening to wear on my finger, he did not notice the translucent skin beneath, the blue flashing veins that ran under and out of the bridge of gold (Emphasis added).... Telling me to go to sleep while he worked at his papers, he did not give another thought to me.... It is his hardness - no, no, not hardness, but the distance he coldly keeps from me. His coldness, his coldness, and incessant talk of cups of tea and philosophy in order not to hear me talk and talking reveal myself. It is that my loneliness in this house (Cry, the Peacock, p.45)."*

This example certainly gives us an idea of Anita Desai's art of reading woman's psychic self, which reveals Maya's inner thoughts. Maya is a hypersensitive woman, an introvert. Many critics have pointed out this incompatibility. Usha Pathania tracing the cause of disharmony between he characters remark: "Marital relationships are established with the explicit purpose of providing companionship to each other. However, the element of companionship is sadly missing in the relationship between Maya and Gautama."(p.45).

Maya on the one extreme is fragile, with deep cultural roots and refined sensibilities. On the other extreme is her friend Pom who absolutely does not bother and is a typical woman with love for clothes, jewellery, colour, looks. newness, for brightness, colour and gaiety. Maya describes her as living in her painted world where there were no shadows of family, tradition and superstition.

There is an identification of Maya with the Peacocks that represent for her cries of love which simultaneously invite their death. Like her, they are the creatures of exotic, wild and will not rest till they have danced to their death. For her, they represent the evolutionary instinct of struggle for survival. She describes how they dance and the remarkable impact produced on her mind, peacocks searching for mates, peacocks tearing themselves to bleeding shreds in the act of love, peacocks screaming with agony at the death of love. The night sky turned to a flurry of peacocks' tails, each star a staring eye.

The dance of the peacock has an intense personal significance for Maya as the peacock destroys each other though madly in love. Her longing for love forces her to kill her husband first and then herself. Anita Desai presents to the readers her opinion about complexity of human relationships as a big contemporary problem and human condition. So, she analyses this problem due to shows changing human relationships in her novels. She is a contemporary writer because she considers new themes and knows how to deal with them. Anita Desai takes up significant contemporary issues as the subject matter of her fiction while remaining rooted in the tradition at the same time. She explores the anguish of individuals living in modern society. Desai deals with complexity of human relationships as one of her major themes, which is a universal issue, as it attracts worldwide readers to her novels. She strives to show this problem without any interference. On the other hand, she allows to hear readers who have their judgment about her novels, characters and action.

> *"Superstitions, all that I dreaded now. I was certain she hated such talks as much as I did, even if she had no reason to fear them. Such things simply did not step over the bright enameled horizon of her painted world, for such things bore shadows, and shadows were alien to her .....(P 61)"*

Yet another variety is that of cabaret dancers who earn their livelihood through their bodies, sometimes only by displaying and sometimes by selling them. The cabaret girls in the novel are what have been described in Sanskrit as *Roopa Jeevas* because they live by their beauty. Although the cabaret girls do not have all the qualities of a Gonika, courtscan as described in *Kam Sutra*, yet they have dancing skill with emphasis on showing their fleshy wares. Maya has nothing but disgust for them but they are described well. The female body which has been stock theme of poetry both in English and Sanskrit has been reduced here to a saleable commodity:

> *"Their portruberent posteriors, and of which they made much, arousing chuckles of delight....bouncing movement that made her bosom more prominent.....so that more and more and more of that white, tallow flesh would rear out of her*

> *blouse.... With a little provocative upthrust of her rump, etc., Their provocative display and movements such as though says, "See what I have? Like it? take it, gentleman, take it, it's yours!".....* "Beautiful! B-beautiful b-bitch! (P. 85).*"*

Another character in the novel is Maya's friend Leila who has married a tubercular man against the wishes of her parents. She is a teacher in a girls' school. She married a man knowing his disease. Her attitude towards life is fatalistic. She is a contrast to Pom. In her fatalism there is a masochistic strain. Desai aptly comments that she "was one of those who require a cross, cannot walk without one" (CP, P.58).

If Maya is obsessed with the albino prediction, Leila has accepted her destiny and does not grudge or complain "it was all written in my fate Jong ago." (.p. 59). If Maya is the pampered child, Leila's parenst have broken all relations with her. They "had not seen her, written to her, or in any way communicated with her since the day of her development" (P. 58)

Anita Desai not only explores and portrays the feminine psyche of a common woman but also of the subnormal bordering on abnormal woman. These are the women who because of various factors are under so much of mental stress that they cannot be called insane, but what comes to our mind is that of Maya who is hypersensitive dreads that she would lose her mental balance and when she is so much lost in herself without moving for a long time. Gautama says :

> *""Still sitting there? You haven't stirred out? Haven't lifted up a book, your sewing? Nothing at*

> *all? But this is madness, Maya" "Madness?" I screamed, leaping up at him, to strike him, to stab him.....and began to cry hysterically (P. 178).* "

Although we are informed just after this that Maya is not sure whether the event actually took place but what is certain is her mental chaos. Through the use of unpleasant animal imagery, Anita Desai depicts the neurotic state of her mind. The impression given is that of mental fever when she sees weird things. The image of a lizard, a repulsive creature, has been repeated in the novel. For example, in Chapter VI we find, the imagery reveals a sick mind. The image of lizard occurs again after two pages. This time the image is realistic but later it is followed by another weird image of rats which clearly suggests Maya's mental breakdown:

> "*And yet, in the neck of the lizard spanned above me on the celing, its pulse throbbed, and seemed a giant pulse for so small a creature, beating furiously as though it were holding its breath till its blood boiled And then, in the very height of stillness, its tail switched. One small, brief twitch But I saw it, and immediately a thousand rats twitched their tails-long, gray, erm-ridden. Just one, before they were still again, stiff (p. 183).* "

There are several other examples of such weird animal imagery used for externalizing the mental state of Maya. Later in the novel after she gad pushed off Gautama from the roof top she goes back to her father's house in Lucknow. She retreats into the world of her childhood, absolutely cut-off from the present reality. She becomes a girl again lost in her world of picture books and toys. This mental retrogression suggests that Maya has not been able to adjust herself in the world of reality and after killing her husband, she mentally goes back to her protected and pampered childhood, the best part of her life. Thus in the character of Maya, Anita Desai has presented the feminine psyche of both a girl and a woman.

Anita Desai studies the inner life of her characters but she never allows them to forget their social and familial ties. Maya looks at her brother, father and husband to save her from this psychological predicament and cries, " Father! Brother! Husband! Who is my savior? I am in need of one. I am dying, and I am in love with living. I am in love and I am dying." (P 84) The quest of Desai's protagonist is not only one woman's quest but the quest of a human being towards some understanding and acceptance of her predicament. Though there are other women in this novel apart from Maya but hers is the heart- rendering story. Nila, Gautama's sister and his mother, these two are the women who symbolically present positivity and strength. Nina has the ability to fight the odds which come into her life. Her view of life as presented by the novelist is "After ten years with that rabbit I married, I have learnt to do everything myself." (P 135) As far as Gautama's mother is there, she is more concerned with her social work than the crying need of lonely Maya who asks her to stay for some more time with her.

The novel's beginning itself brings to the front the theme of husband-wife alienation by unfolding the relationship of Maya and Gautama. Maya, an introvert, daughter of a wealthy artistic father, is married to an older man, detached, sober, industrious lawyer. They are complete opposite. Their married life is punctuated all along by "matrimonial silences" (P 12). What pains her most is her "loneliness in this house". (P 9) A restlessness always boils within her. She feels "defenseless and utterly alone in the company of the bleak, comfortless figure passing as her husband" (P 212). The alienation between them is rooted essentially in his philosophical detachment, which Maya brushes aside. Her rootless keeps on increasing every day. The treatment of alienation is a major thematic preoccupation with Indo-English novelists. Alienation occupies a particularly important place in the works of the later novelists. Their protagonists are like Existentialist heroes, nomads "alienated from nature and society."(P 213).

The protagonists are misfits in their society largely because of certain defects in themselves or due to some evils in the society. The Indo-English novelist is not so much interested in making philosophical statements as in presenting the plight of an alienated individual and expressing compassion for him and disapproval for society. But in this novel Desai presents the silence, solitude, meloncholy and dark world of shadows in Maya's life. *Cry, the Peacock* is concerned with its chief protagonist Maya's Psychological problems. Based on the mythological and archetypal images and symbols, this novel explores the hidden and dormant impulses of Maya's psyche. As a young sensitive girl, Maya desires to love and to be loved. She marries the friend of her father, Gautama, who is much older than herself. She belongs to a traditional Brahmin family which believes in astrology and other prophetic strains of Brahmanical order. On the other hand, Gautama family represents the rational side
of life.

The novelist has thus highlighted the female predicament in various aspects. She excels, particularly in elaborating the miserable position of highly sensitive and emotional women tortured by negligence and loneliness. Certainly the novel is about Maya but all the secondary characters like Nila, Pom, Leila, the mother etc. contribute to the poly timbered voice of the women and the issues related to them.

Thus through the psychic analysis of her characters, Desai is digging deep into the everyday domestic and feminine life each Indian woman goes through, rich or poor, pampered or neglected once more showing us how different the life of a man is from his common, insulted, silent, neglected counterpart-his wife!

> *"Child-like serenity of the girl, Maya, who sat somewhere upstairs, delightedly opening cupboards, pulling out drawers, falling upon picture-books and photographs with high, shrill cries of pleasure hugging them to her, dancing around the room with them, on airborne feet (p. 212-13)."*

The identity crises of the protagonist Maya, stems from several interrelated factors. She is a passionate and sensitive young girl married to her lawyer father's friend Gautama. Being a practical minded person detached from emotions, he is totally antithetical to her. The marriage was never fruitful and Maya slowly turns into psychopath whose emotional needs were seen to be colliding with that of the extremely practical outlook of her husband. The climax of the story lies when Maya's attachment with her father further develops in to an Electra complex which again acts as the catalyst in the following of her marital relationship with her husband.

The hyper sensitive mind of women is illustrated by Desai in the tenderest way where the atmosphere of tension is set ideally against the backdrop of a sultry Indian summer. In the *Cry, the Peacock*, Anita Desai finally leaves it to the readers to complete the story. The oppression and depression, the anxiety and fear, the frustration and foiling of the female protagonist set against a typical Indian scenario brings out the very best of the writers in a coherent way.

Anita Desai's novels and short stories evoke characters, events and moods with recourse to a rich use of visual imaginary and details, which has led to comparisons with the modernist sensibilities of T.S Eliot, William Faulkner and Virginia Woolf.

Most of Desai's protagonists are alienated characters. She portrays her characters as individuals "facing single-handed, the ferocious assaults of existence" (The Times of India) Thus, characters in her novels are generally neurotic females, highly sensitive and engaged with their dreams and imagination, and alienated from their environments. They often differ in their opinions from others and embark on long voyages of contemplation, in order to find the meaning of their existence. That is why they suffer from their relationships more than others do.In other words, in Desai's novels, the love encounters explode into marital disputes as the result of devastating post-marriage relationship between husband and wife.

The marital life of Maya which is punctuated all along by "matrimonial silences" alienates her. She aspires for the life that would permit her to touch him, feel his flesh and hair; hold and then tighten her hold on him. Stemming from marital discord, her alienation ends with severe insanity.

The jarring notes of discontent and frustration in marriage often emanate from temperamental incompatibilities. Maya the emotional, sensitive and impulsive wife is contrasted with the rational, matter of fact, practical husband Gautama. Maya's moods, obsessions, dilemmas and abnormality are conveyed very effectively in the novel. Disenchanted with life for different reasons they become neurotic and the gradual descent to the role of murderers is carefully patterned. Maya's act of murder, is an act of self-liberation.

The communication and comprehension gap between Maya and Gautama is too deep and too broad to be bridged by good intentions or even by intense love. Maya's fascination for the babies in the pigeon's nest suggests her longing for motherhood. Maya longs for motherhood .Aloneness and inactivity destroys the spirit of an individual. In the absence of any activity, Maya gets obsessed with her past and broods over the coldness of Gautama.

Desai's Maya experiences psychic disturbances due to severe demands on their personality. We come across despair, frustration, loneliness and fear in Maya and the psychological states give way to hallucination, thoughts of death that culminate in her final killing of Gautama.

To sum-up, Maya's tragedy is mainly caused by her loneliness, lack of proper response from her husband, non-reciprocation of feeling between the husband and wife, her childlessness and her hypersensitivity.

It is heartening to state that the women novelists constitute a major group of the Indian writers in English. They are now enjoying an increasing popularity and prestige. They have an impressive record of success. They have produced sufficient work to merit attention. The anthology has been confined to fiction for it is in this area feet of the women writers have made a mark on the contemporary Indian literary scene.

CHAPTER THREE

BYE- BYE, BLACKBIRD

Indian women novelists project woman as the central figure by giving a distinct dimension to their image in the family and society. Their insight into the woman's reactions and responses, problems and perplexities and the complex working of their inner selves and their emotional involvement and disturbances enabled these novelists to succeed in presenting the predicament of women most effectively. The existential struggle to establish one's identity, to assert one's individuality, fight to exist as a separate identity, cultural conflicts, the social and economic changes, the problem of the expatriates and immigrants and the personal relationships especially between man and wife are some of the common themes that appear in the novels of Indian women novelists. We find the fullest expression of women's problems through display of various themes in the novels of Anita Desai

Indian couple, like Donne's lovers, together make a world of their own. Each is incomplete without the other. In a Hindu family no religious rite can be performed by a spouse without another. Though a man and a woman become complementary to each other through marriage, there is no certainty regarding their mutual love for each other.

Bye-Bye, Black bird (1971) Anita Desai's third novel has a different theme from the earlier novels. It explores in the main, the immigrant sensibility via a new foreign culture and the consequent problems of adjustment, belonging, roots, past etc. The novel acquires added significance as it examines the questions of east west encounters and cross cultural relationships.

The novel *Bye- Bye, Blackbird* is mainly woven round two groups of characters, viz, Adit Sen, his English wife Sarah, the Indian friend Dev; and Jasbir – Mala, Sammar – Bella. If Maya suffers because of Psychological alienation, Sarah of *Bye-Bye, Blackbird* (1971) suffers because of cultural alienation. The novel portrays the problems of Indian immigrants in London. The title refers to England's bidding farewell to an Indian – a "blackbird". One is reminded of Kipling's view that the East is East and the West is West: and that the twain shall never meet. What is more significant, from a feminist perspective, is that East or West, woman is the underdog and the novel underscores this aspect as well.

Adit's wife Sarah has the most deserving claim to be the protagonist. Here Dev starts moving around in London like a tourist observing and enjoying its various attractions and allurements. He begins to undergo a slow change from Anglophobia to Anglophilia. Later Adit's attitude towards England undergoes a sea change. His Anglophilia gives way to a sudden and disturbing nostalgia for his home land.

Through a few flash-backs, the readers are told about the love affair of Adit Sen with Sarah. Christine Longford, a friend of Adit, introduces Sarah to Adit in a cocktail party. Even in the first meeting. Sarah's shyness attracts him and he chooses Sarah for company because "You re like a Bengali girl. Bengali women are like that, reserved, quiet.

May be you were one in your previous life. But you are improving on it –you are so much prettiest" (*Bye-Bye, Blackbird*, P 73). Except this, nothing is known about their love affair. After their marriage, they settle down in Clapham, a small city. Adit and Sarah have to adjust much because of their different cultures. To satisfy Adit, Sarah cooks Indian foods. But the typical Indian male-chauvinist in Adit finds pleasure in ill-treating Sarah : "These English wives are quite manageable really, you know. Not as fierce as they look – very quiet and hard-working as long as you treat them right and roar at them regularly once or twice a week" (*Bye-Bye, Blackbird, P 29*). Sarah, as a typical submissive wife, on the other hand, always speaks good of her husband. She pretends that she is treated nicely by her husband. When Sarah's Mother asks about her cooking, she says: "Adit Still does most of it" (P 133).

Explaining the cultural incompatibility, Krishnamoorthy Althai observes : "the rituals and beliefs of the one mean nothing to the other, which makes each of them groan in pain at the lack of regard shown by the other, for what each holds dear" (P 104). In the course of time Sarah completely alienates herself from the public and private life. In the school where she works, she avoids conversation with her colleagues who often discuss her married life. Her colleagues wonder how she is able to adjust with the Indian husband. She avoids their probing questions. She loves India. She knows something about India through the pictures of Indian stamps. She slowly changes herself. So that she can adjust with Adit's small matters. She stops cooking English food and learns to cook Indian food. After marrying Adit sen Sarah feels that she is nameless.

> *""She had so little command over these two canoed*
> *she played each day, one in the morning at the*
> *school and one in the evening a home, that she could*
> *not even tell with how much sincerity she played one*
> *role as the other. they were roles-and when she was*
> *not playing them, she was nobody her face was only*
> *mask, her body only a costume ..... staring out of*
> *the window at the chimneypots and the clouds, she*
> *wondered if Sarah has any existence at all, and then*
> *she wondered with great sadness, if she would ever*
> *be allowed to stop off the stage, leave the theatre*
> *and enter the real world-whether English or Indian,*
> *she did not care, she wanted only its sincerity, its*
> *truth" (P 34-35). "*

As the "other", Sarah sacrifices a lot and she is treated like the "other" by Adit Seema Jeha looks at this predicament of Sarah from a wider perspective:" Anitha Desai draws our attention to the annihilation of self that marriage involves, for a female."(*Voice and Vision of Anita Desai, P 47*)

Adit, naturally, is a typical male-chauvinist. He never cares for his wife and her sentiments. Almost all the decisions in their family life are taken by Adit. Without consulting Sarah, he decides to return to India so that "My son will be born in India" (204). Sarah is a passive victim," the other" in the hands of the male-chauvinistic Adit, ironically, when Adit prepares himself and Sarah to leave England, Sarah gets a promotion. When Sarah informs Adit about it, Adit gets angry and accuses Sarah that she does not want to leave England whereas she has already decided not to accept promotion. The discussion leads to a confrontation and Sarah begins to weep. She seems to be more an Indian wife than a English woman. Usha Bande explains the sources of Sarah's alienation :

Sarah in *Bye-Bye, Blackbird* is a case of both social and psychological alienation. "The social factor stems from her marriage to an Indian settled in England; her psychological trouble emanates from her pride system". (The Novels of AnitaDesai, P 119).

Sarah's existentialist dilemma reaches its peak at the end of the novel. Her inner conflict is the result of three problems; one pursuing Adit on his voyage to the East , second holding back to cradle and comfort the uneasy, unborn child and the third tackling the exigencies of a career that had surprisingly revealed a future. After her marriage, she has sacrificed many things to buy peace in her family life. Now she has to say good-bye to England itself where she has lived for twenty-four years.

The end of the novel suggests a peaceful conclusion: "Sarah and Adit held hands like a pair of children, feeling Bengal, feeling India sweep into their room like a flooded river ,drowning all that had been English in it"(224). In a man woman relationship there would be a need for sacrifice and surrender .But the paradox is in reality ,it is always the woman who does so. Hari Mohan Prasad compares Sarah to a volcano: "Sarah's character has more power. In her there is a real split, a real dilemma, a real suffering, but she triumphs over all these. She is a silent volcano, not dead, yet not bursting." (Journal of Indian writing in English, vol.1X No .2.P 64). The irony is Sarah never bursts in the novel.

Adit, Sarah and Dev are highly sensitive and have been amenable to the sanskars of their respective root places. Adit appears to show the typical male dominant character of Indian husbands. He forgot that Sarah was such a genuine, educated western lady, trying to cook Indian food and to please him.

Anita Desai is concerned with the delineation of psychological reality. Hence she prefers the characters who are peculiar and eccentric rather than general and common place. She conceives each character as a mystery and riddle. She believes that it is the duty of a novelist to solve this riddle. Her characters are almost sick of life and listless plaything of their morbid psychic longings. Most of her female protagonists are abnormally sensitive and usually solitary to the point of being neurotic.

> *"She was still breathing hard at having so narrowly escaped having to answer personal questions. It would have wrecked her for the whole day to have to discuss Adit with Julia, with Miss Pimm, in this sane, chalk dusted, workday office. She was willing to listen for hours to Miss Pimm's diagnosis of her aches and pains... But to display her letters from India, to discuss her Indian husband, would have forced her to parade like an impostor, to make claims to a life, an identity that she did not herself feel to be her own, although they would have been more than ready to believe her. (Bye- Bye, Blackbird. P 4)"*

Sarah's problem is human. She wants to be a real person whether English or Indian. She is fed –up with sitting on the fence. She tries her best to remain a sincere wife seeing to it that her marital life is not destroyed. Her husband too had been playing charade although not as consciously as she. But he also realizes falsity of his existence in England and Sarah also knows it well: "His whole personality seemed to her to have cracked apart into an unbearable number of disjointed pieces, rattling together noisily and disharmoniously" (Bye, 200). When after the 1965 Indo-Pak war Adit is in the process of making a decision to leave England for good, he is very edgy and unstable and this is the time when he needs a cooperative and understanding wife, and Sarah does well as a wife. Of all wives in Anita Desai's novels she is the best in understanding and supports her husband.

In the circumstance mentioned above she knows how to handle her husband:

> *"She could not tell what effect the smaller refusal or contradiction might have on him. Rather she would sacrifice anything at all, in order to maintain, however superficially, a semblance of order and discipline in her house, in her relationship with him. His whole personality seemed to her to have cracked apart ... if she allowed this chaos to reflect upon their marriage, she knew its fragments would not remain jangling together but would scatter, drift and crumble.(Bye P 200)"*

Sarah, the English wife of Adit Sen has the same feeling of alienation as her husband. Sarah's dilemma is not that of finding new roots but it is that of uprootedness and hence deeper. She finds herself an alien and a stranger. At the time of her departure, Sarah is sad to leave her place, "It was her English self that was receding and fading and dying, she knew, it was her English self to which she must say good-bye." (Bye P 221)

Like all other Desai's female characters, in this book also, treatment and domestic life of woman is the same, whether set in India or England, Desai unravels the tortuous involution of sensibility with subtlety and fineness and her ability to evoke the changing aspects of nature watched with human moods through the psychological trauma experienced by her female characters.

The main forte of Desai's fiction is the exploration of the main currents and undercurrents of human psyche. She is more concerned with the portrayal of inner reality than the outer life. The struggle of the characters, especially women, to maintain their identity and to emerge as individuals in their own right leads to maladjustment with those who are related to them. Desai's women characters are sensitive and they try their best to cope with their situation in ways that are sometimes damaging to themselves and sometimes to others, because they are often guided by impulse rather than reason.

This novel deals with the treatment of the psychic tumult of her self-afflicted characters. The treatment of the characters is quite different from her earlier novels. In this novel Desai presents the typical problem of adjustment faced by black immigrants in England. She analyses this critical problem by portraying the three major characters, Adit, Sarah and Dev and exploring the effect of racial malice and hatred on their sensibility. These three characters face the dilemma of finding their identity because their background is rooted in the different classes of society divided by birth, and from a definite sense of social placement they find themselves in an alien atmosphere where it is not easy for an individual to adjust.

Anita Desai herself confesses in her article that "Their (immigrants) Schizophrenia amused me while I was with them and continued to tease me when I returned to India. I wrote it in an effort to understand the split psychology, the double loyalties of the immigrants."(Contemporary Indian

Literature,XIII, 1973)

After marriage Sarah's reticence turns into aloofness, she loses her zeal to participate in living and becomes apathetic. She feels that her life is an empty and ineffectual one and therefore is left with stark loneliness. Her bewilderment and frustration is the consequence of 'cultural shock'. Her immersion in a strange culture causes a breakdown in communication, a misreading of reality and inability to cope. Sarah feels depressed because she cannot fully involve herself in her husband's culture nor can she adapt herself to his society. The novelist displays commendable skill in delving deep into her psyche and highlighting her social and psychological isolation. Sarah, like Maya and Monisha, is an introvert, but there is hardly any other kinship between them. She does not suffer from inner vacuity like them though she is temporarily isolated. Mrs. Desai's depiction of Sarah's personality, full of dualities and uncertainties, presents a vivid image of the struggles of an alienated self. Fear, insecurity and the resultant withdrawal are the three major motifs in the novel.

The novel incorporates the impact of an East-West marriage on the psyche of Sarah. As the likings and tastes of husband-wife are different, a disharmony prevails in Sarah's family life and it seems to threaten her marriage. One gets the impression that Sarah and Adit have adjusted to each other despite their differences. His romantic love for England is matched with the romanticism of her imagination about India. They maintain their cultural identities yet experience a close affinity with each other's culture. But Sarah has a dread of being labelled an Indian and there in lies the crux of her difficulty. Her sense of shame and nervousness is so obvious that some readers tend to agree with her colleague.

Julia bluntly says that if being an Indian was so adherent to her, she should not have married, Sarah's irrational fear is not an out come of her social position but in the first place it is alienation only. We can analyze her motives in the light of her anxiety behind her psychological upheaval. At last we can say that *Bye-Bye, Blackbird* deals

with the theme of psychological conflict encountered by the Indian immigrants in England on account of their inability to adjust with the atmosphere and situations alien to them.

The novelist analyses this existential predicament by delineating realistically the situations of three major characters Dev, Adit and Sarah, who fail to come under the terms of reality and consequently feel rootless and utterly cut off from the people around them and also from their own selves.

CHAPTER FOUR

WHERE SHALL WE GO THIS SUMMER

"*Man and wife do not, as a rule, live together they only breakfast together, dine together, and sleep in the same room. In most cases the woman knows nothing of the man's working life and he knows nothing of her working life (he calls it her home life)*

(Bernard Shaw, Prefaces-11)."

Anita Desai is one of the major voices in modern Indian English fiction, K.R. Shrinivasa Iyengar stated.

"*The first two novels of Anita Desai Cry, the Peacock and voices in the city have added a new dimension to the achievement of the Indian women writers in English. This dimension takes multiple forms.(IWE, P 64)*"

If Maya suffers from Psychological alienation and Sarah from cultural alienation, the sense of alienation experienced by Sita, *in Where Shall We Go This Summer,* is difficult to explain. Sita, the protagonist is a married woman in her forties, a mother of four children, pregnant for the fifth time, living in a Bombay flat with her husband Raman, an upper middle class factory owner.

The novel *Where Shall We Go This Summer* (1975) deals with a distracted wife looking to break out her matrimony. The plot follows Sita as she arrives on the pastoral island of Manori after a twenty year absence. She has brought along two of her four children, having abandoned the others with her businessman - husband in their home in Bombay. In the third trimester of yet another pregnancy and convinced that the world is hopelessly nurtured by cruelty and violence, Sita has returned to the island because she believes that it possesses magical powers which can safely terminate her pregnancy.

Now the problem is that she does not want the child to be born. Nor does she like to abort it. Her quixotic wish is that she should keep it safely in her womb and prevent it from being born into this wicked world. Raman is unable to understand her unusual idea. Their level of understanding is not the same. Raman is pragmatic and outspoken whereas Sita is an introvert. Sita is a sensitive woman very much alive to the happenings around her, the cruel violence, that she finds in the human and non-human world around her. She suffers from the existential predicament.

Women's writing continues to occupy a place of importance for more reasons than one. It projects the responses of more than half of humanity and reflects a consciousness constructed by gender. Women's writing has questioned the existing viewpoints which are essentially patriarchal. All women's writing need not necessarily be feminist. But feminist interpretations can emerge through absence and negation. The sufferings of Indian women, marital disharmony, existentialism, anger, dual tradition are the major themes of feminist writing. Female quest for identity has been a pet theme for many a woman novelist. Marital discord recurs as the theme of the novels of Anita Desai. Her novels, with a touch of feminist concern, portray the failed marriage relationship which often leads to alienation and loneliness of the characters. Her novels, like, *Cry, the Peacock, Where Shall We Go This Summer, Voices in the City,* and *Bye-Bye, Blackbird* also deal with the theme of alienation and emotional stress.

Sita's character is analyzed through three different parts of the novel. Part one describes her present life. She is vexed of her husband's passive behavior. She considers the world wicked and be hopeful of escaping from the hasty surroundings. She doesn't like her fifth baby born and face these destructions. With these musings of keeping the baby unborn, she leaves the urban house and goes to the magic land. Manori with her children Menaka and Karan. Part two deals with the past – Sita's life at Manori. She remembers her life in Manori before twenty years. She remembers her life before marriage. Everybody had great respect in her father. He set an ashram in his house and many followed his ideals. He is a saint to his disciples and a magic man to the villagers. Part three, the final part shows her coming back. It analyzes her mental state by drawing a parallel between her fancies and the reality. Her children who were accustomed to the urban life could not adjust in the island. Her daughter writes a letter to her father and they go back to Bombay. The significant thing throughout the novel is Sita's wisdom. Despite the tensed moments she has always been conscious of her surroundings. Her insightful movements made her achieve the right path. Sita could not even treat her husband's friends, guests, and visitors with tolerance.

They appeared to her like animals. Later she could analyze the contrast, the life in Bombay and her imaginary world. She says, "I should have known how to channel my thoughts and feelings, how to put them to use. I should have given my life some shape then some meaning. When she remembers her childhood, she remembers how she used to live in her small world which had given her solace – being an escape from her inabilities. This skill of analyzing situation shows her matured self perceived later. Her responsible nature is observed when she thought of taking care of her children on her own, despite the hallucinations, loneliness and restlessness in her existence. In this novel, Sita's own attitude to married life must have been warped by the knowledge and experiences in regard to their parents. The cause of her unhappiness is rooted in the miserable and lonely childhood. Her mother ran away to Benares leaving her husband and children behind and gave no information about herself. She was deprived of her mother's affection and her father also failed to look after his children. Moreover, his incestuous attraction for Sita's elder step-sister Rekha must have shocked and the disclosure that Rekha is not her real sister also gives her upset.

Thus we see that the claim of intuition and the process of reason are at clash in *Where Shall We Go This Summer*. Forty- five - year old Sita is the mother of four children and pregnant with a fifth. But the vital link, the mother is missing in her. She desperately tries to belong to something but is isolated. Sita's crazy refusal to bring her fifth child indicates her despair. It grows out of the fear that the outer reality will crush her existence. She loses her inner identity which excludes her from all meaningful rationality. She feels that by escaping to the island of her childhood she will be able to carry out her mission. So she goes to the island of Manori .

In *Where Shall We Go This Summer,* Sita shifts from compliance to rebellion and then to withdrawal, again coming back to compliance. Since she oscillates between her changing strategies, her behavior is inconsistent and leaves much scope for disparity between her thinking and actions. In the first part of the novel, entitled *Monsoon* 67, she rebels against her family and decides to go to Manori "What I'm doing is trying to escape from the madeness here, escape to a place where it might be possible to be same again" (35) – The second part *winter* 47 depicts Sita's life twenty years back, her life with her father.This part enables us to understand her later conflicts. Alternatively, her resigned and aggressive trends dominate the third section *Monsoon* 67 (106).

Sita's husband, Raman is the son of her father's friend (a situation similar to Maya & Gautama). When Sita's father died, Raman took her from the island, sent her to college, and – because it was inevitable- married her. As she recollects, when Raman came to take her away, he closed the theatrical era of her life and led her – out of the ruined theatre – into the thin sunlight of the ordinary, the everyday, the empty and the meaningless life. It is in those terms – "empty" and "meaningless" that she views her married life from which she derives no satisfaction.

The temperamental incompatibility between Raman & Sita is brought out through a number of incidents in the novel. Raman, for instance, sees no meaning in Sita trying desperately to save a wounded eagle from the crows: "They've made a good job of your eagle' said her husband, coming out with his morning cup of tea. He laughed and asked her to look at the feathers sticking out of that crow's beak. She cried that perhaps it flew away, knowing it had not. In this novel too the central character Sita is a free but isolated individual who is solely responsible for her own actions and reactions. This way, *Where Shall We Go This Summer* deals with the facts of the life and explores the sensibility of Sita.

Sita is physically unimpressive and over – sensitive. Her over-sensitiveness does not allow her to mingle with an ordinary life. It compels her to go away from this burdensome and crowded area. Sita decides to flee to Manori where there is no crowd except natural scenery. Her over – sensitiveness does not allow her to give birth to her fifth child. She wishes to say a positive, no. But her stay at Manori helps her to understand that she cannot live forever on a make believe stage and that she has to accept her existence as a whole.

Sita, the protagonist of this novel like the legendary Sita, had spent many crucial years of her life on the island of her childhood, Manori. The modern Raman, unlike the legendary Raman does not understand his wife. The marital discord of the modern Rama and Sita is ironically referred with that of the idealized relationship that existed between the legendary Rama and Sita even though the similarity in names and situations is clearly seen as accidental. Marriage does not seem to offer Raman and Sita any solution rather aggravate the situation severely. They lead their life like an ill-assorted couple by lacking altogether in harmony in their lives and their marriage bond is proved to be unions of incompatibility.

Sita feels herself to be a prisoner in a house which offers her nothing but a crust of dull actions and of hopeless disappointment. Living with her rational husband, she finds her surroundings too unpleasant and cruel to cope with. Her reactions like smoking, abusing her children for trifles and getting extremely angry when the servants talk in the kitchen shows her hypersensitivity. She then decides foolishly not to give birth to the fifth child in a world of violence and develops hatred for the world. She cries and says, "I don't want to have the baby" (30). She further says, "I mean I want to keep it. I don't want it to be born in this desolate and overly meaningless world"(31). Madhusudan Prasad observes that this novel deals: "A recurrent existential theme that lies bare in the agonized modern sensibility of an Indian woman" (25).

The interrogation used as the title of the novel, *Where Shall We Go This Summer* leaves a big question mark. The name itself is suggestive of an escape from the summer that stands for the raging inner tension, frustration, disappointment, mental discord and disharmony of the inner consciousness of Sita. Anita Desai views the violence through the eyes of a woman in the limited area of her domestic relationship. Desai concludes this novel with Sita's recovery from her plunge into existential reality. Sita as a "broken bird" of the seashore analyzes the cause of her anxiety and neurotic behavior and learns to cultivate the art of survival in the destined life. Her triumph over her illusions renders the island devoid of its powers and miracles

The study of isolation experienced by women in male dominated society is a significant modern trend. In the Indian society woman are not allowed to play any active role in decision-making. They are ignored or brushed aside. In such situation Anita Desai tries to focus on the predicament of women in the society. Most of the women created by Anita Desai have some trait or the other which psychologists would love to analyse. They strikingly appear as individuals and gradually get subsumed as types of women in conflict with their environment. Such types of women are ubiquitous.

Desai's mother characters are not traditional, self effacing women. Sita for instance, revolutionizes the concept of motherhood by refusing to give birth to her child in a hostile world. Preoccupation with the fragmentation of reality and its impact on the human psyche is of continued interest to Desai in all her major works. She tries to explore and convey truth which she associates with the mind and not with the body. She distinguishes clearly between truth and reality.

Anita Desai is specially noted for her sensitive portrayal of the inner life of the female characters. Several of Desai's novels explore tensions among family members and the alienation of middle-class women. She explores the intricate facts of human experience bearing upon the central experience of psychic tensions of characters. Her chief concern is human relationship. Her central theme is the existential predicament of an individual which she projects through incompatible couples – very sensitive wives and ill matched husbands.

Thus, Anita Desai's female characters go through traumatic experiences in their incompatible martial bonds that push them into an emotional deprivation. The women of Desai's novels seek a serene state of loneliness in order to fly away from the suffocation that the society impels on them.

In this novel, Desai follows the track of Bronte sisters, who chose to study the heart and mind of women from women's point of view. These novels provide glimpses into the tortured souls of their heroins. In like manner Anita too portrays the tragic intensity of her women characters with a feminist perspective. This novel depicts the tragic life of Sita who leads a life of isolation and loneliness in her husband's house. Her unmitigated suffering drives her to a state of madness and desperation. Desai portrays her women characters as sentimental and introspective under the influence of British women novelists Meredith, George Eliot, Virginia Woolf and Richardson.

The conflict between the need to withdraw in order to preserve one's wholeness and sanity and the need to be involved in the painful process of life is shown vividly in the novel. This wavering between attachment and detachment reflects the need for a meaningful life. Psychological experiment of the writer in the novel can also be seen on the portrayal of Sita's character. Psychologists attach great significance to the parent-child relationship, because, according to them the patterning of emotion takes place particularly during childhood. They argue that the prevailing quality of the experience the child has with his parents particularly the mother during early childhood is of paramount importance.

Childhood is the most formative period of one's life.Personality and socialization of the child begin in the family in the company of his parents who are the first individuals with whom the child interacts. Child learns the patterns of behavior which the parents set out to teach him in order to make him an acceptable member of the society. The emotion of the child depends largely on the quality of the emotional interaction that prevails between the child and his parents. Anita Desai's characters have strange childhood, and their experiences and interactions during this formative period when combined with their congenital hypersensitivity contribute towards their inability to establish and maintain harmonious inter-personal relationship in later life.

Anita Desai tries to show the anxiety of Sita who suffers because of her biased attitude towards life. Sita is over-sensitive who finds herself confined in the urban life after leading a carefree life in rural area under the protection of her father. The artificialities, fast pace and harshness of city life nauseate her to such an extent that she longs to go back to island where she has cherished all the delicacies of rural life and where she thinks her roots are. After being taken away from her father and her place, she feels the void and expects more love and care from her husband Raman.

She feels insecure and finds everything wrong with Raman He had nothing more to give her, or he was just unaware of her needs and demands. He raised his hand and stroked Karan's hair with a gentleness she herself ached to attract, and stared at him, bored into him with her eyes, wanting and not being given what she wanted. (*Where Shall We Go This Summer* P 132)

Sita is a symbol of nature and cannot adjust with the mechanical world. She seems to be an 'odd one' where she is alienated from her family and society. She is upset by the sight of crows feeding on a young eagle. Immediately she rushes for a toy gun of Karan and uses it on the crows to keep them away fromthe poor eagle. The husband wife alienation forms the basis of the novel as Raman and Sita differ a lot in their temperaments. Sita always accuses Raman for his lack of understanding and Raman, could never understand the emotional state of Sita and he considers her deeds as immature and foolish ones. Sita appears to be a woman of contradictory thoughts. She is a woman of complex character and even Raman, her husband could not understand her.

"You must stay where there is a doctor, a Hospital, and a telephone. You can't go to the island in the middle of the monsoon. You can't have a baby there.(33)"

Family plays a vital role in the growth and development of individual and broken homes definitely has its worse effect on an individual. Sita is one such victim who because of her bitter experiences in her childhood alienates herself from everything around her. Sita's character has been portrayed in such a way that it represents the predicament of a modern married woman in the society. She initially escapes from reality and later reconciles to the circumstances.

Sita's life is re-defined in the island. She realizes that her own married life and all other relationship around her are based on a compromise in their duties and selfishness and this is the cause of ugliness, disharmony and increasing violence in life. She accepts reality of life instead of illusions. Unlike Maya in *Cry, the Peacock,* Sita comes out of her illusionary world. Maya always thinks about the childhood prophecy of disaster. But Sita realizes her mistake in the magic island. Her voyage ends with the discovery that she has some responsibilities in her life. She also discovers her hidden aspects of her real life. So, the illusionary world gives way to her real world and her duties. Desai views through the eyes of her female protagonists that everyone has some duties or responsibilities in their life. They must accept it in any way. In fact, her visit to Manori helps Sita to fuse into one the span of present, past and future and life-span of childhood, youth and adult age. She redefines her relationship with her childhood soil, Manori. There is also a change in Sita's identity and she is redefining her relationship with her husband. She understands her husband and decides to go with him. Sita, therefore, return to the mainland with a sense of renewed awareness with reality rather than live in the illusory dream world like Manori.

Anita Desai's novels are certainly reflective of socials realities. But she does not dwell like others on social issues. She digs deep into the forces that condition the growth of a female in this patriarchal male dominated society. She observes social realities from a psychological perspective without posing herself as a social reformer. Her novels are studies of the inner life of characters and her talent lies in the description of minute things that are usually unnoticed. The researcher has chosen the Psycho Analytical Method for this dissertation because it is interesting to study how complex a human mind is and how differently different characters react to the same situation.

The interaction between past and present is a typical narrative device which Desai has used to convey the constant mental activity that characterizes human beings and also compensates for the limited external action. Sita's compromise marks a progression from Maya's insanity and Monisha's suicide, brings the narrative's philosophical approach to existence more into evidence -an approach that recommends a synthesis of emotion and intellect.

Though the country has made a lot of progress, the role of Indian women in society remains only peripheral. Gender discrimination has been a universal phenomenon in human history from time immemorial. Owing to a new set of educational values and economic dependence, the position of women has certainly been enhanced and women have now certainly got a status in society. But in order to iron out the unevenness in society, they need to learn to assert their rights and shun the injustices heaped on them. Thus the new generation of Indian women novelists advocates independence and assertiveness in women by depicting their characters as survivors who successfully bear torment both physical and emotional and raise a voice against the brutalities and violence surrounding them. They tend to rebuke the male dominating Indian society which discourages self-reliance in women and urge women to build up their fragmented lives and express their affirmation.

Anita Desai's novels thus occupy a unique place in Indian English Literature as invaluable works of psychological study of Indian women's inner life from a feminist perspective along with the process of alienation they undergo as a part of their emotional and social changes, Sita too is not different though she acquires practical wisdom at the end of the novel. Desai's novels are thus a reflection of the disturbed psyche of women who are victims of alienation and male dominance. However, they find a way out by self-discovery and introspection.

CHAPTER FIVE

SUMMING UP

"A woman should be aware of self controlled, strong-willed, self-reliant and rational, having faith in the inner strength of Women-hood. A meaningful change can be brought only from within by being free in the deeper psychic sense . (A Married Woman, Manju Kapoor)"

The twentieth century has seen a host of female writers, in India, taking up the cause of the woman who is searching for ways to assert her selfhood in a society that is prejudiced in favour of man. They are courageous enough to renounce the pattern of female expression set by age-old patriarchal codes of behaviour by showing protagonists with the courage to fight, modify or transform themselves.

These writers help to break the image of the mentally suffering Indian woman. One of the prominent modern writers among them is Anita Desai, who is a novelist endowed with an unusual sensibility and an unrelenting will to fight for the cause of women by projecting them in a sympathetic light in novel after novel. Women especially married women hold centre stage in her novels and all of them are presented as pictures of suffering in one way or another. Despite various laws and constitutional rights the Indian woman continues to be defined in terms of man and regarded as subordinate to him.

With western education the horizon of the Indian woman has extended beyond her family and her exposure to the world has opened her eyes to the iniquity and oppression that society exercises on her in the guise of tradition. Traditional rules of conduct have hitherto smothered her spirit and now she has begun to revolt feeling trapped in the tentacles of a society, and started to either use her pen or her voice as weapon against it.

Anita Desai in many ways, is a representative of Indian women novelists in English whose contribution to fiction is more significant than the other women novelists, such as Kamala Markandaya, Ruthprawar Jhabavala, Nayantara Sehgal. She is not one of those Indian writers who cater to the westerner's demand for information about the Indian scene or Indian thought but to pour out their soul and reveal their vision into reality only to share it with other people. She, evolved from a time when the sapling of renaissance in India had grown into a banyan tree. Its branches spread in all directions. Those were the days of conflict between the old and the new, of rebellion against modernity. Anita Desai's writing presents a fascinating study of human beings torn within and outside. Her characters do have a rare appeal which lies in their highly articulated psychological actuality.

Anita Desai has carved women's character in her art with her social awareness and she portrays many issues that middle class Indian women undergo in a power structured, male dominated Indian society. In Desai's novels over pampering or rejection in childhood creates psychological locks in the way to maturity in healthy inter- personal relationship in adult life. Desai's protagonists turn the whole face of romance upside down. The girl marries the boy according to her parent's choice, slowly measures him in terms of her intellect and finds him inadequate and therefore takes her own path--murder and turning insane (Maya), suicide (Monisha), or taking to the life of a recluse (Sita, Nanda). In short Desai's novels present the ceaseless quest for a meaningful life by the modern, educated, sensitive women. To Desai's protagonists. marriage means annihilation of their selves.

Anita Desai has sought to examine the whole range of relationships in her characters and this essentially shapes the thematic value of all her novels. She has explored these relationships with a remarkable intensity and consistency. Anita Desai deals with 'individual' rather than 'society'. She has left the known world of social documentation and skipped the stage of domesticated novels. While the earlier women novelists have confined them to the domestic life of their characters, she goes much further and ventures to explore the inner thoughts and feelings of her characters (Vasanji 2008). Anita Desai, being a woman herself, is naturally inclined to delve on the plight of women in the male dominated Indian society. She tries to depict the intensity of human sufferings. seen in the limited context of family, she lays emphasis on the values of the individuals. Anita Desai is especially noted for her sensitive portrayal of the inner life of her female characters. Several of Desai's novels explore tensions between the family members and the alienation of middle-class women.

In her later novels Desai has dealt with such themes as German anti – Semitism, the devise of traditions and western stereotypical views of India. In this close context of co-existence, mutual respect, mutual understanding and enthusiastic attitude to help each other, and also in the backdrop of relationship crises, let us take up the themes of Anita Desai's major novels.

A novelist may claim to be highly objective and imaginative; yet he or she is bound to be subjective and autobiographical to some extent, as his or her own experiences and observations may get reflected in his or her writing. According to D.H. Lawrence: "The author never escapes from himself. he pads along within the vicious circle of himself. There is hardly a writer living who gets out of the vicious circle of himself or a painter either" (*Phoenix: Posthumous Papers of D.H.Lawrence* P 180). In Anita Desai's novels the themes of alienation, racial and cultural conflict between traditionalism and modernism, have an unmistakable echo of the autobiographical considering the fact that Desai's protagonists are either born and brought up in india or living a mixed type of life outside india. Characters Maya. Monisha, Sarah, Sita, Amla, Nirode etc reflect to a certain extent their creator, what she has already experienced or desired to experience. In her interview with Yashodhara Dalmia, she admits:

> "*In countless small ways the scenes and settings certainly belong to my life. But the major characters and the major events are either entirely imaginary or an amalgamation of several characters and happenings. (Times of India, 29 April 1979)*"

Anita Desai's masterpiece 'Cry the Peacock' is a typically feminine novel, not because it is a story of a woman told by a woman but because it is the fruit of feminine sensibility. In the novel, Desai presents Maya as the dissenting woman who battles against three traditional forces in her life; male authority expressed by her husband; her female friends who play stereotype-submissive-wife roles and; her religious belief in karma. Here, the central focus is steadily laid on 'Maya' the female protagonist and the disintegration of her psyche under a variety of pressures; the chief of which is marital discard or temperamental incompatibility. "I am and I am in love with living, I am in love and I am dying. God, let me sleep Forget, rest. But no, I will never sleep again. There is no rest any more –only death and waiting."(CP, 54).

In fact *Cry, the Peacock* is a psychological study of how a young and sensitive married woman is desperately ruined by marriage. Maya showering love on her dog, reaches the height of intensity to bring an end to her husband's life at her own hands, she initiates the existence of Anita Desai's sensitive heroines in harsh and cold world, dominated by men, who search for value and harmony in life and either annihilate themselves or compromise with their destiny (Desai, 1980, CP).

Desai's characters value rights and they measure their spouses in comparison to their model figures. She aids in lack of communication between husband and wife in most of her novels and this lies as the fundamental problem for all failed marriages.

Childhood plays a very important part in the development of an individual. A child's relation with his parents deserves special mention. In Anita Desai's novels, the parent-child bond is never satisfying; either the parents are over-indulgent and over-possessive. or the child experiences total rejection. Most often children find their parents as a model on whom to shape their characters. But unfortunately in some of Desai's novels, the children are left with a single parent as in *Cry, the Peacock, Where Shall*

We Go This Summer, or their relationship with their parents does not satisfy their emotional needs. Sita, who is rejected by her parents at a very early age. has a negative attitude towards life. This negative relation with her parents in her childhood leads her to have the same negative relation with her children too.

In Desai's *Where Shall We Go This Summer*, Raman is an ideal husband and father. The children love him; finally he agrees with Sita that the island is not so bad a place and that they could live together on the island. This positive step by Raman brings changes in Sita, who reconciles and returns with him to the city. Desai shows that for an ideal family life, both husband and wife have to play equal share and that without adapting to each other's behavioral patterns, life will not be pleasant.

Desai is more interested in her characters and the story is of secondary importance. However the most common theme in Desai's novels is the complexity of human relationships, particularly the man-woman relationship.

The theme has been as old as the novel itself and can be found in Richardson, Fielding, D.H. Lawerence, Virginia Woolf, Hemingway and Faulkner. Emphasizing the importance of such a relationship, D.H. Lawerence in "Morality and the Novel" points out:

> "*The great relationship for humanity will always be the relation between man and woman. The relation between man and man. Woman and woman parent and child will always be subsidiary. (130)*"

Desai's novels are Psychological. Instead of presenting man in conflict with the society. Desai wishes to keep her focus on man in conflict with his mind. In *Cry, the Peacock*, Desai explores the consciousness of Maya, who is intensely involved with life, her fears of impending death, her loneliness and her longing for love. The first and last parts of the novel are in the third person narrative, whereas the middle part is in the first person and is full of poetic passages and flashbacks. The three parts deal with the three stages of Maya's neurosis—growth, development and climax. Her dialogues are natural and meaningful. The novel *Where Shall We Go This Summer* reveals Desai's superb mastery of the stream of consciousness technique which is obviously her strongest forte and which has been so frequently resorted to in almost all her novels. Throughout the novel Desai makes an effort to probe deeper into the complex inner life of its protagonist Sita.

The major dominating themes in Anita Desai's novels are, the sense of alienation and detachment and human relationship particularly the man-woman relationship. Nowadays these kinds of themes have assumed special significance in the closer context of rapid industrialization, growing awareness among women of their rights and individualism, and the westernization of attitudes and lives of people Literature for her is not a means of escaping reality but an exploration and an inquiry. She prefers the private to the public world and avoids the traditional grooves of external reality and physical world. In fact, her real concern is the thorough investigation of human psyche, inner climate, and she unravels the mystery of the inner life of her characters. She writes neither for placing entertainment nor for dissemination and propagation of social ideas. Her main engagement is to study human existence and human predicament, her exploration being a quest for self. *"She is the novelist of psycho-emotional situations and her theme is the individual against himself and against the milieu*" (*Manmohan K. Bhatnagar*: 110). This particular reality leads to the most common theme in her novels that is the complexity of human relationships, particularly the man-woman relationship.

Anita Desai explores the Indians' (especially women's) use of make-shifts to escape attachment and their attempt to find love and life in disillusion that are the end product of their alienation, obsession, transgression and diffusion of self in double consciousness, i.e., of a woman and then an Indian.

The uniqueness of Anita Desai's fiction, however, lies in her treatment of feminine sensibility. In India where women have redesigned roles, which do not allow any room for individualism, identity and assertion, Anita Desai advocates for women who question the age-old traditions and want to seek individual growth. They try to reassess the known in a new context and find a meaning in life.

Most of Desai's protagonists are alienated characters. She portrays her characters as individuals "facing single-handed, the ferocious assaults of existence"(*The Times of India*) Thus, characters in her novels are generally neurotic females, highly sensitive and engaged with their dreams and imagination, and alienated from their environments. They often differ in their opinions from others and embark on long voyages of contemplation, in order to find the meaning of their existence. That is why they suffer from their relationships more than others do. In other words, in Desai's novels, the love encounters explode into marital disputes as the result of devastating post-marriage relationship between husband and wife.

Anita Desai has dwelt upon problems of love, marriage and sex in her novels in a very convincing and realistic way. She seems to champion the view that marriage alone does not provide a ready-made solution to life's tension, chaos and turbulence. Instead, mental satisfaction and happy married life means better understanding between husband and wife.

One needs the genuine help of the other. A proven and trusted sense of co-operation at every stage and phase is required. Psychological adjustment is safe key to a healthy compromise and cordial existence in a conjugal life. Husband and wife need to nurture the strong feeling that they are complimentary to each other.

The theme of alienation is treated in terms of mother-children relationship which itself is a consequence of dissonance in husband-wife relationship.

Where Shall We Go This Summer(1975) has been applauded as "an interesting addition to Anita Desai's achievement as an Indian novelist writing in English" (Vimla Rao P 50). In this novel, Desai pinpoints "a real and pathetic picture of a lovely married woman and aspires to establish victory over the chaos and sufferings of her rather unusual existence" (Vinay Dubey P 5). She presents her favorite theme of investigating the consciousness of an introvert and sensitive woman who is bored and frustrated by her commonplace and hum-drum life and tries to escape into purposeless and unproductive loneliness. She chooses marital discord as the subject matter and highlights how the inability to lay bare one's soul and one's fear and anguish results in the snapping of communication between husband and wife. Different attitudes, individual complexes and fears add to this distancing between the husband Raman and the wife Sita resulting in conjugal disharmony. Structurally this novel seems to have been inspired by Virginia Woolf's masterpiece *To the Lighthouse*.

Throughout the novel, Desai makes a meticulous attempt to go deeper into the extraordinary inner life of its protagonist, Sita. Here she reveals the character of Sita through the stream of consciousness method, with layers of thought in her mind. Sita and Raman, like Mrs. and Mr. Ramsay who stand poles apart from each other, have irreconcilable temperaments and attitudes to life. The ill-assorted couple is confronted

with the same problem of husband-wife discord. Sita represents a world of emotion and feminine sensibility while Raman is a man with an active view of life and the sense of the practical. Sita is a nervous, sensitive middle-aged woman with explosive and emotional reactions to many things that happen to her. She always wants to escape realities and she even hesitates to perform ordinary responsibilities of life. She finds her very existence threatened with boredom because her husband keeps himself busy in his business and the children growing independent.

On the contrary, Raman represents the prose of life. He represents sanity, rationality and an acceptance of the norms and values of society. He is unable to understand the violence and passion with which Sita reacts against every incident. His reaction to his wife's frequent outbursts is a mixture of astonishment, weariness, fear and finally a resigned acceptance of her abnormality. He cannot comprehend her boredom, her frustration with her existence:

> *"... she herself looking on it saw it stretched out so vast, so flat, so deep, that in fright scrambled about it, searching for a few of these moments that proclaimed her still alive, not quite drowned and*

dead. (Where Shall We Go This Summer:P 33)."

In this novel, again, the theme of alienation and lack of communication in married life is discussed and re-assessed by the writer. Sita finds herself alienated from her husband and children. She remains an ignored personality since childhood. She is the product of a broken family. She yearns to have the attention and love of others, but her father remains busy with his chelas and patients. Even after marriage, she remains lonely. Her husband also is busy. He fails to address her expectations. As a result, there is marital discord, a widening gulf and increasing tension between husband and wife.

Bye-Bye, Blackbird is the story of many Asians who seek out greener pastures in the western world. Fed up with the state of things in their country, they move out into foreign shores only to be disillusioned at the cold reception they get there. It does not matter whether one is an Indian or a Pakistani or a Bangladeshi – all are grouped together as Asiatic and looked down upon as they make their cities dirty and polluted. The novel is the story of Adit and Dev, two immigrants to London. Adit comes from a well-to-do educated Bengali family in Calcutta. He does try to find a job in his native place but the nature of his clerical job with all its dinginess, unpunctuality and slowness puts him off. He gets back to London and marries an English girl Sarah and incorporates all English manners and values in himself. The latest immigrant is Dev, his friend who has gone there to study at the London School of Economics and is appalled to see the way the Asians are treated with no one even protesting. Hereon, there is a reversal of roles and situations. Adit prepares to come back home with his wife whereas Dev reconciles with the demeaning situation and comes to terms with the alluringly bright side of London. Sarah also creditably, pushes her English identity into the background and willingly gets ready to be assimilated into the new culture.

The experience of exile has assumed mythic proportions in commonwealth literature. It begins as a condition of living and intensifies as a condition of the mind. Its broad sources are cultural displacement and cultural shock. Cultural displacement implies a co-presence of more than one culture-biculturalism or multiculturalism: multiculturalism is now a world phenomenon, biculturalism, a shaping commonwealth reality. In fact all the countries that have had the misfortune of being colonised have to experience the traumatic searing of the self. India had a glorious cultural heritage that dates much earlier to the Vedic period. But the impact of the Western World, through nearly three centuries of British colonization .Also the Portuguese, the French and the Dutch brought forth new patterns of cultural behavioural value system which have generated tension in the society. Tension arising from the tradition versus modernity, Indian *Vs* Western, dwindling of the conventional value system, ambivalent cultural response to the West, socio-economic disparities, and colonial consciousness as a hangover of the British rule.

The characters in Anita Desai's novels try not to revolt or participate in any kind of activism but rather seeking the freedom of the mind, spirit and the body from their surrounding in a peaceful way. In her fictional exploration of the individual female consciousness, Anita Desai in effect opposes the traditional Hindu conception of identity which is communal rather than individual. She creates characters that are sensitive, introspective and individualistic to the point of eccentricity, so that they emerge as misfits in the conventional environments in which they are placed.

Desai's sharp awareness of the inner reality and the massing of details is expressed in a manner that the interior self of the characters is revealed in all its prominent shades. Her protagonists are not average. In this chapter the researcher has described such sensitive souls as, sweet Sarah in *Bye-Bye, Blackbird*. All the protagonists in Desai's novels were undergoing mental conflict of varying intensity. Some of them are lost during the struggle, while others come out successfully with new realization and hope.

The main forte of Desai's fiction is the exploration of the main currents and undercurrents of human psyche. She is more concerned with the portrayal of inner reality than the outer life. The different states of mind produce different reactions in different situations. In the world of Desai's character there is an amalgamation of all types of human psyche. Various factors give rise to mental tension of varying intensity. Most prominent among the causes of these mental conflicts is the clash between the inner reality of the protagonist and the external situation of their life.

The protagonists of Desai suffer from these mental agonies at various levels. They often come in clash with the outside life, with others at individual level, or with the society at-large. The changes brought in their mental perspective with the time and experience also produce a psychic strain. Mostly the female protagonists are usually more sensitive than their counterparts but sometimes as in the case of Raman in *Where Shall We Go This Summer,* we find that men can be sensitive too. In this chapter the researcher tries to analyze alienation and psycho analysis of the Female protagonists in Desai's three selected novels *Bye-Bye,Blackbird, Cry, the Peacock and Where Shall We Go This Summer*. These novels are replete with instances of psychological conflict.

In Bye-Bye, Blackbird, published in 1971, Desai widens her canvas to deal with a group of Indian immigrants in London and in her sensitive manner traces their complex emotional relationship. It is different from the other novels by Desai in an important aspect that is while the other novels have an Indian setting, but *Bye-Bye Blackbird* is set in an English background. But whatever the setting, a constant theme in Desai's novels is the problem of adjustment, both personal and social. At the personal level, the problem is more complex. The struggle of the characters, especially women, to maintain their identity and to emerge as individuals in their own right leads to maladjustment with those who are related to them. Desai's women characters are, who are sensitive can try as best to cope with their situation in ways that are sometimes damaging to themselves and sometimes to others, because they are often guided by impulse rather than reason.

Desai's heroines live in a tightly enclosed world and inevitably their repression breaks out in violence. In *Cry, the Peacock*, Maya murders her husband and becomes insane, Monisha in *Voices in the City* commits suicide and Raka in *Fire on the Mountain* sets the forests ablaze. *Bye-Bye Blackbird* though written in digression from the track, on which the earlier novels of Anita Desai move successfully on the theme of existential isolation and lack of adjustment encountered by Indian immigrants in England.

This novel deals with the treatment of the psychic tumult of her self-afflicted characters. The treatment of the characters is quite different from her earlier novels.

In this novel Anita Desai presents the topical problem of adjustment faced by black immigrants in England. She analyses this critical problem by portraying the three major characters, Adit, Sarah and Dev and exploring the effect of racial malice and hatred on their sensibility. These three characters face the dilemma of finding their identity because their background is rooted in the different classes of society divided by birth, and from a definite sense of social placement they find themselves in an alien atmosphere where it is not easy for an individual to adjust.

Anita Desai herself confesses in an article: "Their (immigrants) Schizophrenia amused me while I was with them and continued to tease me when I returned to India. I wrote it in an effort to understand the split psychology, the double loyalties of the immigrants".

Anita Desai is not quite satisfied with this novel, as it presents the plight of Indian immigrants in an alien land too realistically. Dev feels isolated in London from both Indians and Englishmen because the former have become used to the condescending attitudes and motives which he cannot follow, and the latter consider him an outsider. At the beginning Adit is happy but later on he feels isolated and his attitude towards England undergoes a major change. Dr. G.D. Barke has rightly said:

Adit though lives and admires England, loves everything that is English appreciates her history and poetry, feels the thrill about Nelson's battles, waterloo, about Churchill all, and yet all this break like a soap bubble at the first touch of reality. He must have not loves England less but then he loved India more. (Barke, GD, P 234)

His initial anglophobia is ultimately supplanted totally by his new experienced anglophobia. He considers himself to be a stranger and a misfit in England. He moves about

London in a kind of morbid search for belonging. Sarah, Adit's wife, though not deeply involved in the main motif of the novel, she is also an existentialist character suffering from the feeling of isolation and loss of identity. She also feels upset because by marrying an Indian she feels alienated in her own country.

The novel opens with the arrival of Dev in England. He is a young student, with some intellectual pretensions, from Bengal, desirous of taking admission in the prestigious London school of Economics. He finds himself totally a misfit in England because he is unable to reconcile with the English norms and conventions and finds it difficult to adjust in an alien land. The novelist powerfully and effectively narrates the various experiences that Dev undergoes and the culture shocks that he receives in a foreign country. He remains one of those, " . . . eternal immigrants who can never accept their new home and continue to walk the streets like strangers in enemy territory, frozen, listless, but dutifully trying to be busy, an unobtrusive and, however superficially to belong . . ."(Barke.GD P 5) as he has read a long about it in books. The self-consciousness that leads him to a self-crisis around which the whole novel revolves, the crisis is not peculiarly Dev's own.

It seems to have a much larger dimension; it seems to overpower all those who are placed in similar situations. If it engulfs Dev, it also engulfs Adit, and his English wife, Sarah. Dev cannot get accustomed to the quietness and an emptiness of London city. He experiences a lack of sympathy and geniality among the British who cannot recognize even their neighbours and live like strangers to one another. The discovery of artificiality in manners, lack of ethics and morality among the British preys upon his mind constantly. Though now and then, he enjoys the idyllic countryside but on the whole he does not feel at home with this new locality and resides there like an unwanted, isolated and insulted creature. The humiliating treatment accorded to immigrants in England, hunts him. While travelling in a bus, he feels humiliated while buying his ticket for seats a glint of scorn in the conductor's eye, the abrupt way in which he hands him his ticket and then keeps him waiting for his change. Even the old lady sitting next to him clutches her handbag and leans away from him as if she finds him repulsive.

The novel revolves around the crisis of identity that the characters have to face. Living in uncertainty, denied and rejected, Dev develops a schizophrenic attitude towards England. However, in the final section of the novel we observe that Dev loses his self control and is slowly drawn into London life. The English countryside stirs his inner self, lets him open his soul and fills it with that healing touch which nature along can give and Dev as he responds to the scenic beauty of English countryside rediscovers the magic that he had lost in London. Thus, Dev who feels depressed in the early stages of his stay in London because of the insults hurled at the black by the callous and arrogant British, gradually finds the life of an alien enthrallingly rich and highly enterprising. Adit's situation is just the opposite of Dev's. In the beginning he is Anglophilliac, marries an English girl Sarah and settles in England with no desire to return to India. He is often ridiculed by Dev, as a "spineless imperialist lover," but unlike Dev he is happy there because he understands the reconciliation between the two different cultures the Eastern and the Western, the meeting of discordant natures and backgrounds. A vein of sarcasm and irony underlines the analytical thoughts of Adit, but he manages to solve his dilemma of the Indian mind's fascination for the western culture.

Adit settles down in England because he fails to find a decent job in India in spite of having a degree from a British University. With a little difficulty he finds a job as a travel agent and is generally content with life. Like his fellow immigrants, he quietly tolerates racial insults and humiliations to which he is continually subjected. Fed on English Literature in school and exposed directly to English life and manners for years, he now feels a sense of cultural affinity. This closeness, however, does not obliterate the sense of his cultural identity. He secretly longs for Indian food, music and friends. This longing suddenly grows intense during one of his visits to Sarah's parents. Adit, from then onwards, feels stifled and starved in the alien land. He makes up his mind to leave for India to lead a real life clear of all pretences.

We are informed with the help of a few flashbacks how the marriage between Sarah and Adit is materialized. To Sarah, Adit seemed a complete contract to her. She had been brought up in a strict and drab atmosphere which was in sharp contrast to Adit whose life seemed colourful drab in contrast to England's social atmosphere. The novel deals, at great length, with the numerous adjustments which a married couple is compelled to make or fails to do so. Adit cannot stand British broth and stews and, therefore, he makes Sarah to cook Indian food immediately after marriage. Since she is not able to cook Indian food to the entire satisfaction of her husband most of the time, Adit is found in the kitchen which irritates his mother. Sarah and Adit have difficulty in adjusting to each other's concept of cleanliness also. Sarah takes no precaution to protect the food from the cat sniffing at it and Adit's appetite is killed when he thinks of eating the unclean food. Adit's Bengali music has no impact on Sarah.

She cannot join him and his Indian friends in their conversation, jokes and laughter, and thus remains a foreigner in their world. She does not find it easy to wear a sari and Indian jewellery. The rituals and beliefs of one mean nothing to the other, which upsets both of them at the lack of regard shown by the other, for what each holds dear. A major part of the book is devoted to husband – wife isolation. After marriage Sarah's reticence turns into aloofness, she loses her zeal to participate in living and becomes apathetic. She feels that her life is an empty and ineffectual one and therefore is left with stark loneliness.

Her bewilderment and frustration is the consequence of 'cultural shock'. Her immersion in a strange culture causes a breakdown in communication, a misreading of reality and inability to cope. The theme of psychic deviations and cultural alienation is common in the 20th century literary scene. Lost, lonely, drifting characters parade before us and their mechanical march point to the absence of meaningful relationship in the era of technological development and global interaction. It has become a universal phenomenon. Anita Desai gives a graphic picture of this and alienation of uprooted individuals in the novels. Desai reads the minds and understands the fact that they are suffering from alienation. Her characters in *Bye-Bye, Black Bird* become victims of these feelings.

As an expert, Desai portrays the ontological insecurity, alternation and anguish of uprooted individuals in her novels. Her alienation of this problem is prevalent in most of her works. She remarks her conditions as "This has brought two separate stands into my life. My roots are divided because of the Indian soil on which I grew and

European culture which I inherited from my mother".(Desai, Anita. The Book I Enjoyed writing most. *Contemporary Indian Literature*, XIII, 1973,P 24).

Anita Desai's preoccupation as a novelist has been the exile alienation of characters. Each of her novels presents one or two memorable characters. In the character portrayal again, she is primarily interested in the projection of female protagonists living in separate, closed, sequestered worlds of existential problems and passions, loves and hates. Unlike most of Indo-English novelists, Anita Desai does something unique by portraying each of her individuals as an unsolved mystery. Her concern for the character alienation enables her to offer an unexpected glimpse into the deeper psychic state of her protagonists. She says:

> *"I am interested in characters who are not average but have retreated, or been driven into some extremity of despair and so turned against, or made a stand against, the general current. It is easy to flow with the current, it makes no demands, and it costs no effort. But those who cannot follow it, whose heart cries out "the great No," who fight the current and struggle against it, they know what the demands are and what it costs to meet them. (Anita Desai in her interview with Yashodhara Dalmia, The Times of India, Sunday Bulletin, April 29, 1979."*

The above study of the novels shows that even though socially Desai's protagonists Sarah, Sita and Maya are not very happy because of racial prejudice and alienation from her people yet as a wife they very sensibly take care of things. Most of Anita Desai's couples don't pull well in marriage but happily here we have a warm understanding wife, that is Sarah. Her social being may not be satisfied and contented. We have all-out praise for this alien woman who understands her husband, his family and country which she would accept, once in India. Anita Desai very brilliantly has brought to focus the exile and self-alienation of three characters in *Bye-Bye,Black Bird* namely Adit, Sarah and Dev. The uprooted individuals Adit, Dev and Sarah have constant identity crises and suffer from exile, cultural and social alienation throughout the novel. The researcher has tried to present the growth of the exile literature from its humble beginnings to its status in the present day.

Anita Desai's female characters are not interested in changing the reality and the world in which they live but all that they want is to prove that they are human individuals and that they will not surrender their individuality. The prime concern of the authors is the married woman and her circumscribed world where she has a very precarious existence. The lack of security in marriage and the consequent confinement within a self-enclosed world have degenerated women into emotional beggars. While Desai presents characters like Maya. Sita. Sarah who quite passively accept their dependent, inferior status in marriage, being unable to find support from within themselves or from other broader interests; and cling on shamelessly to their husbands, pathetically grateful for the random moments of companionship.

In analyzing the predicament of the married women Desai traces the causes to their very childhood experiences and seem to suggest, like Bala Kothandaraman, that the "child is mother of the woman" (38). Though they do not have many child protagonists, they look very seriously into the childhood of their mature women protagonists and analyse their childhood experiences in the backdrop of their present status in life. The stress they give to the childhood of their characters reveals their conviction that all of them carry the legacy of their disturbed childhoods into their married lives and also seems to suggest the need to impart due care and love to their practical husbands.

The Portrayal of feminine psyche is a pervading strain in all Anita Desai's monumental works. These novels basically express the frustration and disappointments of women who experience the social and cultural oppression in the male-dominated society. It highlights the agony and trauma experienced by women in male-dominated and tradition bound society. These novels unravel the tortuous involution of sensibility with subtlety and fineness and her ability to evoke the changing aspects of nature matched with human moods is her asset. If Desai's fiction is able to advance from the vision of loneliness as a psychological state of mind to that of alienation as a metaphysical enigma-her writings may one day achieve an amplified pattern of significant exploration of consciousness comparable to Virginia Woolf at her best.

The novels *Bye-Bye, Blackbird, Where Shall We Go This Summer* and *Cry, the Peacock* dealt with theinner psychic conflicts of their female protagonists and also the theme of alienation both they and their counterparts suffer. The author has beautifully presented the irony of human life i.e, after a time of rejuvenation one should return to their reality of life. Although they continue to live together, the husband and wife do not share anything between them not even the sensibility that can differentiate between half-sweet, half-sad fragrance of petunias and some astringent smell of lemon. They find their temperaments

irreconcilable. Woman whether in England or in India faces
loneliness and most times husbands fail to recognise the
inner conflict their wives undergo.

Works Cited

Primary sources

Desai, Anita. *Bye-Bye, Black Bird*, Delhi: Orient Paperbacks, 1985.

Desai, Anita. *Cry, the Peacock*. London, Rupa Paperbacks: 1963

Desai, Anita. Where shall we go the summer - New Delhi, Vikas, 1975

Secondary sources

Baig, Tara Ali: *India's Women Power*, New Delhi, S. Chand, (1976).

Barke, G.D. *"A Study of Alienation in Bye-Bye Blackbird and The Strange Case of Billy Biswas" Critical Essays on Anita Desai's Fiction*. Ed.

Desai, Anita. *"The Book I Enjoyed Writing Most"*, *Contemporary Indian Literature*, XIII, No. 4, Oct.-Dec. 1973, p. 24.

Desai, Anita. *"The Book I Enjoyed Writing Most"*, *Contemporary Indian Literature*, XIII, 4, 1973.

Desai, Anita. *Bye-Bye Blackbird*, pub. Orient Paperbacks, Delhi, 1985, p. 32. 6. Ibid., p. 72.

Desai, Anita. *In Custody*. Agra: Lakshmi Narain Agarwal.1967.

Desai Anita. In Jackson Elizabeth, *Feminism and Contemporary Indian Women's Writing*. New York :Palgrave McMillan .2010.p.33

Desai, Anita. *Fire on the Mountain*, William Heinemann, London 1977: Allied Publishers, New Delhi, 1977.

Desai, Anita. *Flight of Form*, India International Centre Quarterly, Vol. 10. No. 4, D., 1982.

Desai, Anita. *The Book I Enjoyed Writing Most. Contemporary Indian Literature*, XIII, 1973. Anita Desai in her interview with Yashodhara Dalmia, *The Times of India,* Sunday Bulletin, April 29, 1979.

Deshpande, Shashi : *Literature and Gender*, Directorate of Distance Education, MDU, Rohtak, 2004.

Dubbe, P.D. "Feminine Consciousness in Anita Desai's *Fire on the Mountain".* *Critical Essays on Anita Desai's Fiction*, ed. Jaydipsingh Dodiya Pub. IVY, Publishing House, New Delhi, 2000, p. 116 &121.

Gupta, Ramesh Kumar "The Concept of New Woman In Anita Desai's *Clear Light of Day",* *Critical Essay on the Anita Desai's Fiction* ed. Jaydipsingh Dodiya Pub. IVY, Publishing House, New Delhi, 2000, p.153.

Gupta, Vijayanti : *The Guarded Tongue*, Aug. 2003,

Horney, Karan. *The Neurotic Personality of Our Time,* New York: Norton. 1937.

Iyengar, K.R. Srinivas. *Indian Writing In English*. New Delhi: Sterling Publishers, 1993.

J. Krisnamurthy : *Women in Colonial India. Essays on Survival, Work and the State*, Oxford University Press 1989.

Jain, Jasbir. *Anita Desai Indian English Novelist.* Madhusudan Prasad(Ed). New Delhi. Sterling Publishers Pvt.Ltd, 1982.

Jaydipsingh Dodiya Pub. IVY. Publishing House, New Delhi, 2000, p. 93.

Khan, M.Q. and Khan, A.G. : *Changing faces of Women in Indian writing in English*, Creative Books, 1995.

Klein, Ronald : *A Survey of Indian American Writers*, Muse India 2013.

Kumar, Ajit : *Poetic and Social Development in Indian English Poetry*, Vol. I,
Issue-II, April, 2012 www.galaxyimrj.com.

Kumar, Ashok : Portrayal of New Women – A study of Manju Kapur '*A married Women*', India Ink New Delhi, 2002, 1998, P 90.

Kurketi, Sumitra. Love Hate relationship of Expatriates in Anita Desai's *Bye-Bye, Blakbird*, the novels of Anita Desai : A critical study, E d. Bhatnagar & Rajeswar M., New Delhi: Atlantic Publishers and Distributors, 2000.

Lal, Malashri. "Anita Desai: *Fire on the Mountain*", *Major Indian Novels and Evaluations*, ed. N.S. Pradhan, New Delhi, Arnold Heinemann, 1985.

Manawat, B. Dushyant. "Ethnic Love - Hate Relationship in *Bye-Bye Blackbird*". *Critical Essays on Anita Desai's Fiction*, ed. Jaydipsingh Dodiya, pub. IVY, Publishing House, New Delhi, 2000, p. 93.

Monti, Alessandro and Dhawan, R.K. : Discussing Indian Women Writers : Some Feminist Issues, Prestige Books, New Delhi, 2002.

Mukherjee, Meenakshi. "A Review of *Clear Light of Day*", *The Hindustan Times*, 8th Dec., 1980.

Mukherjee, Meenakshi. "The Theme of Displacement In Anita Desai And Kamla Markandaya", *World Literature Written In English,* 17, No. 1, April 1978, pp. 225-33&240.

Parghi, Raju : Indian Drama and the Emergence of Indian Women Play-Wrights : A Brief Survey, Impressions (e-journal) Vol. IV, Issue II, July, 2010.

Ram Atma."Anita Desai: The Novelist who writes For Herself", An Interview by Atma Ram. *The Journal of Indian Writing in English*. Vol. 5 No. 2, July 1977, p. 31.

Rana, Sunita : A Study of Indian English Poetry, International Journal of Scientific and Research Publications Vol. 2, Issue-10, Oct. 2012.

Rani, Usha. *Psychological Conflict in the Fiction of Anita Desai*, Abhishek

Publication Chandigarh, 2006, p. 15,129,203&207.

Rao, P.Malikarjuna and M.Rajeshwar. Indian Fiction in English. *"Feminism in Anita Desai."* New Delhi: Atlantic Publishers and Distributors, 1999.

Rushdie, Salman : The Art of Critical Appreciations of Indian Novelists, Starred Reviews, London, 2008.

Sarangi, Itishri and Mukherjee, Yajnaseni : The Revolutionary Spirit of the Contemporary Women Writers of India, IOSR Journal of Humanities and Social Science Vol. 5, Issue 6 (Nov.-Dec. 2012), PP 19-21.

Saxena, Alka. "The Impending Tragedy in *Fire on the Mountain*", *Critical Essays on Anita Desai's Fiction* ed. Jaydipsingh Dodiya. Pub. IVY, Publishing House, Delhi, 2000, p. 127.

Sethi, Sunil. "Pieces of the Past: Review of *Clear Light of Day*", *India Today*, S.No. 23, Dec. 1-15, 1980.

Sharma, R.S. *Anita Desai Indian Writer Series*, Vol. 18, New Delhi, Arnold, Heinemann, 1971.

Sharma, R.S. Alienation, Accommodation and the Local in Anita Desai's *Bye-Bye, Blackbird, The Literary Criterion,* 1979.

Sharma, Ram (Dr.) : *A History of Indian English Drama*, blog posted on Jan. 24, 2010 Sunoasis Writers Network.

Singh, Kanwar Dinesh ; *Contemporary Indian English Poetry*: *Comparing Male and Female Voices*, Atlantic Publishers and Distributors Jan. 2008.

Szxena, Alka. "The Impending Tragedy in *Fire on the Mountain*". *Critical Essays on Anita Desai's Fiction*, ed.

Jaydipsingh Dodiya Publ. IVY, Publishing House, New Delhi, 2000, p. 124.

Toffler, Alwin. *Future Shock*, London, The Bodlehead. 1970, p. 13.

Tripathi, J.P. *The Mind and Art of Anita Desai*, Bareilly, Prakash Prakash Book Depot, 1986, p. 83. [235]

Wall , Stephen. *A Neurotic Response To A Failed Marriage: George Meredith's Modern Love*. Mosaic XVII/1, winter 1984, p. 51.

Walsh, William. *The Uses of Imagination.Desai, Anita. Where Shall We Go This Summer?* Orient Paper backs. New Delhi: 1982. Print.[2].

Wandrekar, S. Kalpana. *The Ailing Aliens, (A Study of the immigrants in six Indian Novels)*, Gulbarga, J I W E Publications, 1996.